The Compassionate Father:

The World's Greatest Unfinished Short Story

Luke 15:11-32

Eli Landrum

The Compassionate Father: The World's Greatest Unfinished Short Story
ISBN: Softcover 978-1-946478-30-6
Copyright © 2017 by Eli Landrum

All rights reserved. No part of this book may be reproduced or transmitted in any form or by any means, electronic or mechanical, including photocopying, recording, or by any information storage and retrieval system, without permission in writing from the publisher.

To order additional copies of this book, contact:

Parson's Porch Books
1-423-475-7308
www.parsonsporch.com

Parson's Porch Books is an imprint of **Parson's Porch & Book Publishers** in Cleveland, Tennessee, which has double focus. We focus on the needs of creative writers who need a professional publisher to get their work to market, **&** we also focus on the needs of others by sharing our profits with those who struggle in poverty to meet their basic needs of food, clothing, shelter and safety.

To my children and grandchildren with love

Table of Contents

Introduction   7

Scene 1: A Hasty Departure (Luke 15:11-13)   29

Scene 2: A Harsh Reality (Luke 15:14-16)   51

Scene 3: A Moment of Truth (Luke 15:17-20a)   61

Scene 4: A Homecoming (Luke 15:20b-24)   75

Scene 5: A Plea of Impartial Love (Luke 15:25-32)   95

Scene 6: _____   117

Introduction

After a long span of time, I still remember the gist of the story. I read it in the Sunday School quarterly my church provided for boys in my age group. In the story, a young boy came downstairs dressed to go to church services with other family members. This Sunday, however, he was not wearing his usual dress clothes. Instead, he had on casual or everyday clothes, which in my boyhood would have been overalls or blue jeans, a shirt he wore for work or play, and everyday shoes—clod-hoppers, as we called them. His father objected to the boy's attire and told him to go back to his room and put on his Sunday best. The boy explained his reason for what he had chosen to wear. He had invited a friend to attend church with him, but the friend's family was poor and the friend had no Sunday clothes to wear to church. He would feel out of place and ashamed to go to church in the clothes he had. The boy told his father that to put his friend at ease, he would dress as the friend did and accompany him to Sunday School and worship. All these years, I have remembered the lessons of that story, even if I often have failed to practice them: True friendship involves caring, sensitivity, and a willingness to put another's feelings first; concern for another person's spiritual welfare will accommodate itself to that person's needs. A simple story made a lasting impression on me.

Most of us can recall stories that remain meaningful to us, for almost everyone likes a good story. Somewhere, individuals may exist who do not have time for or appreciate stories no matter how gripping, moving, entertaining, or educational they may be. My guess is that such people are few. From childhood, most of us have been drawn to stories, written and oral. Today, we appreciate good stories skilled storytellers tell or write. Good storytellers can make mediocre stories come alive; inept storytellers can butcher excellent stories. Talented storytellers can enable us to experience dramatic stories that are memorable, enriching, and enduring.

Most small children are fascinated by stories geared to their understanding, and as their attention spans lengthen, they will sit in parents' or grandparents' laps, contented and enthralled as the adults read stories. Often, at bedtime, children will ask—or demand—that parents read the same stories over and over.

Children learn the stories, but they still want to hear them read. When our children were small, I sometimes would read only part of a story and say, "The end!" I never got away with it. They knew the story by heart and would not be fooled. For many of us, childhood fondness for good stories carries over into adulthood.

I do not remember being read children's stories, but I do recall grammar school teachers reading stories to at least partially attentive classes. My earliest recollection is that of an elementary school teacher reading *Under the Lilacs* to her class. Somewhere along my way, I was introduced to adventure stories for adolescents, such as the Hardy Boys series of novels. Of course, I became acquainted with Mark Twain's wonderful accounts of the adventures of Tom Sawyer and Huckleberry Finn. At some point or points early in my life, someone—or several individuals—instilled in me a love of reading that has continued to the present.

In our day, books abound. In the words of the writer of Ecclesiastes, "Of making many books there is no end" (Eccles. 12:12, NIV; unless otherwise indicated, quotations from the Scriptures are from the *Holy Bible, New International Version*). Novelists who are good storytellers become famous, rich, and even influential. Louis L'Amour, one of my favorite authors, viewed himself as a storyteller: *"I think of myself in the oral tradition—as a troubadour, a village taleteller, the man in the shadows of the campfire. That's the way I'd like to be remembered—as a storyteller. A good storyteller."*[1] He was an excellent storyteller, as is evidenced by the number of his books still in print long after his death and by a legacy that has continued. He remains the standard by which other writers in his genre—western novels and short stories—often are measured. No doubt you have favorite authors in various genres who tell their stories well, so you look forward eagerly—even impatiently—to their next books.

Movies based on and communicating riveting stories become blockbusters that merit seeing repeatedly; they become timeless in their messages and impact. At the top of my list of favorite movies—and books—is *To Kill a Mockingbird*. Set in a deep south rife with racial prejudice, the story of a brave white lawyer seeking justice for a wrongly accused black man and the repercussions for

---

[1] Louis L'Amour, *Riding for the Brand* (New York: Bantam Books, 1986), 245.

The Compassionate Father

the lawyer and his family has moved me deeply each time I have seen the movie. The perfect casting, the actors' performances, the setting in the south in which I grew up, and the lessons presented for the learning have caused me to see the movie numbers of times. The story's realism and drama continue to stay with me and affect me.

People who tell funny stories quickly gain eager audiences. One of the most fascinating people I have seen and heard was Jerry Clower—the faithful, active Southern Baptist layman who went from being a fertilizer salesman to become one of the best and best-loved country comedians in history. I was in the audience at a Southern Baptist Convention when he courageously challenged Christians to take the lead in working for racial equality when to speak in such a way—even to a Christian audience—involved considerable risk.

As part of his ministry as a Christian layman, Jerry Clower made himself available to speak in churches when he was in Nashville, Tennessee over weekends to perform or to meet with his agent. He spoke to a packed sanctuary in my church. Because I served on the church staff in a part-time position, I had the opportunity to see him up close and to watch him interact with people. He was a huge man—a former college football lineman—and he came across as bigger than life. On another occasion, I happened to be in the Southern Baptist Brotherhood headquarters in Memphis, Tennessee, when he dropped in for a visit and immediately dominated the room. He was a consistently forceful personality.

In his work as a salesman, Jerry Clower had begun telling funny stories at meetings and conferences. People encouraged him to write his stories for publication, but he did not do so. Then someone suggested that he record the stories. He followed through on the suggestion and became famous as a funny man who was determined to demonstrate that a Christian who told clean stories could be a success in show business. He wanted to tell stories families could enjoy. He accomplished his goal in a big way, and he used his fame to impact people for Christ. He did not merely tell funny stories; he told stories in a funny way. He was a great storyteller who mesmerized audiences with good, clean humor.

Another humorous storyteller I remember with gratitude was one of the first people of whom I was aware who chose Christian entertainment as his vocation. Grady Nutt had a rare ability to poke fun at Southern Baptists in a way that made needed and important points without offending his hearers. He could do so because he was a Southern Baptist with a deep love for people. His life ended too soon in a tragic plane crash, but he left a legacy of clean, thought-provoking humor.

Songs that tell brief stories often become popular, sell well, and remain as favorites. Stories set to music can amuse, comfort, and move people emotionally. In His beautiful Irish voice, I heard Daniel O'Donnell sing "Nobody's Child," a story-song about a blind orphan, and it moved me to tears. Both our children are adopted, and I cannot forget the song about a child nobody wanted to adopt

Preachers and other speakers who illustrate well with stories that have clear applications maintain their audiences' rapt attention. In fact, good stories are remembered long after other sermon materials are forgotten. Preachers who can put Bible stories in contemporary terms communicate messages from the Scriptures that have lasting impact. I still recall a revival service I attended as a boy in my small hometown church in which the evangelist, who once had been an actor, presented Jesus' parable of the rich fool in Luke 12:13-21 in terms of my time. I was mesmerized.

By and large, adept storytelling has become somewhat rare, I think. In my childhood, before television sets were commonplace and when not everybody owned a radio, storytelling was an art cultivated on front porches of homes—especially rural homes—where family members, friends, and neighbors often spent hours telling about their youthful experiences, family lore, and the adventures of people they knew. Today, in our hurry-up, get-on-with-it society, most folk have little time to tarry and talk. Thus, when a really skilled storyteller appears on the scene, he or she finds a ready market for an appealing product.

The Power of Parables

No one else has equaled or surpassed Jesus as the supreme master at telling stories. The Gospels contain numerous stories He told as He sought to teach people eternal truths. For years, I have been convinced that we do not have all the stories He told. Yet we have more than enough to gain clear insights concerning Him, God, God's purpose, and ourselves. We call Jesus' stories parables. The word *parable* translates a Greek term that means "a comparison," "a likeness," or "a pithy and instructive saying." The verb from which the noun comes means "to put or cast alongside," "to place one thing by the side of another for the sake of comparison." Behind the Greek word is a Hebrew term that means "parable," "proverb," "byword," or "similitude." Thus, parables range from the short maxims such as the ones presented in the Book of Proverbs to longer stories designed to instruct listeners or readers. All scriptural parables are comparisons designed to make specific points.

Jesus was not the first biblical personality to use parables in the form of brief stories. In Judges 9:7-20, to counter Abimelech's attempt to rule the people of Shechem, Jotham told a story involving trees that searched for a king. They went to an olive tree, a fig tree, and a vine and invited them to become their king, but the olive and fig trees and the vine refused. Finally, the trees approached a thorn bush and invited it to become their king. The story's point was the sheer folly of making Abimelech king.

Perhaps the most notable Old Testament parable is the story the prophet Nathan told King David in 2 Samuel 12:1-10. David had committed adultery with Bathsheba, had arranged for her husband Uriah to be killed, had married Bathsheba, and had thought he was in the clear, home free. Then with amazing courage, Nathan confronted David and told the king about a wealthy man who took a poor man's pet lamb, slaughtered it, and served it to a guest at a meal. The wealthy man's ruthless act enraged King David. At that point, Nathan said to the king: "You are the man!" (2 Sam. 12:7). The prophet's dramatic, pointed story was so effective that David responded: "I have sinned against the Lord" (v. 13). The riveting story, told by a skilled storyteller, painted a king into a corner and drew from him needed confession and repentance.

In Isaiah 5:1-7, the prophet gave a remarkable parable in the form of a song, a poem. It is the story of a vineyard owner who carefully prepared a vineyard in the expectation that it would yield a bumper crop of good grapes, "but it yielded only bad fruit" (v. 2). Through Isaiah, God asked His people what else He could have done for His vineyard—Israel as a nation. Why had His people produced a bad harvest? Because God "looked for justice, but saw bloodshed; for righteousness, but heard cries of distress" (v. 7), He would judge His people. Jesus' parable of the vineyard in Mark

12:1-2 well may be a recasting of the song of the vineyard in Isaiah 5:1-7.

Jeremiah 18:1-12, a classic example of prophetic symbolism, is a marvelous visual parable followed by extensive explanation. God directed Jeremiah to go to the potter's place of work. When he arrived, the potter was busily at work at his wheel. The jar the potter was shaping with the clay became flawed, so he began again and molded the clay into the jar he had in mind. The message was that God was similar to a master potter who had the authority and power to work with His people to shape them into an acceptable vessel. Furthermore, He is the God of second chances—and more.

Jewish rabbis used parables as they taught. One story was about "a king's son who had fallen into evil courses. The king sent his instructor to him with the message, 'Come to thyself, my son.' But the son sent back answer to his father: 'With what face can I return? I am ashamed to come into thy presence.' Thereupon his father sent him word: 'My son, should a son be ashamed to return to his father? If thou returnest will it not be to thy father that thou comest?'"[2] Some scholars see in this parable an echo of Jesus' story in Luke 15:11-32. Any such echo, however, is faint, for the differences in the two parables are pronounced.

Jesus' Use of Parables

Although Jesus was not the first teacher to use parables, He raised the art of storytelling its highest level. No one before Him had employed parables so prolifically or so effectively in teaching. No one since His ministry has come close to matching His skill. His parables include short, pointed statements and longer stories. Interpreters differ on the number of Jesus' parables, depending on their views of what constitutes a parable. R. C. Trench listed and interpreted 30 parables;[3] George A. Buttrick treated 44 stories Jesus told;[4] and Robert L. Cargill found 39 parables.[5] Acknowledging

---

[2] William Barclay, *And Jesus Said* (Edinburgh: The Church of Scotland Youth Committee, 1966), 10-11.
[3] R. C. Trench, *Notes on the Parables of our Lord* (Grand Rapids, Michigan: Baker Book House, 1948)
[4] George A. Buttrick, *The Parables of Jesus* (New York: Harper & Row, Publishers, 1928), xi-xii.
[5] Robert L. Cargill, *All the Parables of Jesus* (Nashville: Broadman Press, 1970), 9-10.

that the number of parables will depend on an interpreter's definition of what a parable is, Archibald M. Hunter wrote: "(Bruce [counted] 33 [parables] plus 8 'parable germs'; Julicher 53; and B. T. D. Smith finds 62.) Our own answer would be: 'about 60.' "[6]

Jesus made wide use of stories in His teaching ministry. In Mark's Gospel, the earliest story Jesus used was in response to some people's question about the reason Jesus' disciples did not fast as did John the Baptist's disciples. Jesus used the figure of a bridegroom to teach that while He was with them, the disciples had no reason to fast. When He was gone, they would fast (Mark 2:19-20). Then Jesus used the figures of a patched garment and of new and old wineskins to emphasize the newness of His teachings (2:21-22).

The first occurrence of the word *parable* in the Gospel of Mark is in 3:23. In response to the teachers of the law who charged that Jesus was possessed by Beelzebub, "the prince of demons" (v. 22), the Lord "spoke to them in parables" (v. 23). In 4:2, Jesus taught "many things by parables" to a crowd by the Sea of Galilee. He told the people the parable of the sower (or soils, vv. 3-8). Later, the disciples and others asked Jesus to explain the parable, and He did so in verses 13-20. In verses 33-34, Mark wrote: "With many similar parables Jesus spoke the word to them, as much as they could understand. He did not say anything to them without using a parable. But when he was alone with his own disciples, he explained everything." These words emphasize Jesus' frequent use of parables to teach spiritual truths.

Jesus introduced His explanation of the parable of the sower (or soils) with words that are difficult and, on the surface, disturbing: "The secret of the kingdom of God has been given to you. But to those on the outside, everything is said in parables, so that,

> "'They may be ever seeing
>   but never perceiving,
> and ever hearing but never
>   understanding;
> otherwise they might turn
>   and be forgiven!'" (Mark 4:11-12).

---

[6] Archibald M. Hunter, *Interpreting the Parables* (Philadelphia: The Westminster Press, 1960), 11.

Jesus quoted Isaiah 6:9-10—God's words to Isaiah when he answered God's call to prophesy to His people. At first glance, the words seem to mean that Jesus used parables to prevent people from understanding His message, repenting, and being forgiven. Jesus' clear purpose, however, was to reveal people's need to repent and to receive God's mercy and grace that were readily available through Jesus. How, then, are we to interpret Jesus' quotation of Isaiah?

James A. Brooks has offered a helpful approach to an understanding of Mark 4:11-12. The word "secret" (v. 11) conveys the idea of truth that once was hidden but now is revealed. The truth Jesus revealed is that in Him, God's kingdom has broken into history. The people closest to Jesus were responding to God's revelation in Him; to people outside—unresponsive or inattentive to Jesus—everything was heard as "parables" or riddles because those people were not open to the truth. A correct understanding of Isaiah 6:9-10 is key to what Jesus meant in Mark 4:12. God told the prophet to proclaim His message even though the people would reject it. "The seeing without perceiving, the hearing without understanding, and the failure to turn and be forgiven . . . were the result, not the purpose, of his message. So, it was also with the parables of Jesus. Therefore, the Greek word *hina* (translated 'so that' in the NIV) at the beginning of v. 12 ought to be translated 'as a result'. . . . Jesus did not speak in parables for the purpose of withholding truth from anyone; but the result of his parables . . . was that most did not understand and respond positively. He did speak in parables to provoke thought and invite commitment."[7] The people who went on rejecting Jesus and His teachings made themselves blind and deaf to truth. They hardened their hearts.

For the most part, Jesus' stories have only one main point. Some, such as the parable of the sower, the seed, and the soils (mentioned above, Mark 4:3-8,13-20), have allegorical elements. That is, elements in the stories have symbolic meanings. Through the years, imaginative minds have viewed all Jesus' stories as allegories and have found all kinds of hidden and far-fetched meanings. For example, Origen, an early church father, interpreted the parable of the Good Samaritan allegorically. "The man who fell among

---

[7] James A. Brooks, "Mark" in *The New American Commentary* (Nashville: Broadman Press, 1991), 83.

thieves is Adam. As Jerusalem represents heaven, so Jericho, to which the traveller (sic) journeyed, is the world. The robbers are man's enemies, the devil and his minions. The priest stands for the Law, the Levite for the prophets. The good Samaritan is Christ himself. The beast on which the wounded man was set, is Christ's body which bears the fallen Adam. The inn is the Church; the two pence, the Father and the Son; and the Samaritan's promise to come again, Christ's Second Advent."[8] To grasp such intricate symbols—to interpret and apply the parables as allegories—the first hearers would have had to have been geniuses; the simple folk who heard Jesus gladly would have had no chance to grasp the stories' well-hidden meanings. Yet Jesus characteristically taught by using parables for the express purpose of making spiritual truths clear, readily understood, and easily applied. His stories were not meant to be mysteries people could solve only through rigorous mental gymnastics or would have to unravel with painstaking effort.

Jesus used common, everyday things and easily recognized people to guide His listeners to deeper levels of spiritual understanding. A farmer sowing his fields, a shepherd tending his sheep, a housewife baking bread, a widow petitioning a judge for justice, a neighbor asking to borrow bread, people who owed others money, wise and foolish builders, a rich man, a tax collector, a Pharisee, a wedding guest—Jesus presented an amazing array of figures who populated the Holy Land. Simple objects such as a coin, bread, seed, a pearl, buried treasure, wineskins, a patch of cloth, a fig tree, money, wheat, and tares became vehicles of spiritual truths. Part of Jesus' genius in His teaching methods was His use of what was familiar to His listeners to hook their interest as He prepared to make His points.

Jesus' parables have been defined as earthly stories with heavenly meanings. To me, this description is much too simplistic and fails to give adequate weight to Jesus' stories. Most assuredly, His parables are comparisons that reveal spiritual truths, but they are much more. They are more than lovely, memorable stories that teach lessons. Jesus' parables called for the first hearers to make life-changing decisions. Today, His stories still call for decisions on the part of readers. The people who first listened to them heard

---

[8] Hunter, *Interpreting the Parables*, 25-26.

implied, underlying questions: "What do you think?" "What will you do with this truth?" "How does this apply to you?" John Claypool offered a marvelous insight into Jesus' parables: "Parables begin as portraits of other people, and then suddenly turn into mirrors in which people see things about themselves that they had not seen before."[9]

Jesus' parables demand that we read with an openness to receive insights and challenges, with a readiness to act on what we receive, and with a willingness to change—to make a commitment to Him. The people who first heard Jesus' stories doubtless left His presence with various reactions. At least a few probably went home wondering, *What does that have to do with anything? I wonder what He meant by that?* Some left thinking they merely had heard lovely, entertaining stories and failed to grasp the underlying, significant spiritual teachings. Others went away having been stirred to see themselves in a new light of truth—to evaluate themselves honestly, repentantly, and contritely. In Jesus' stories, we are forced to face His demands, ourselves, and spiritual truth on which we must act.

Who of Jesus' followers can read the story we commonly call the parable of the Good Samaritan and be comfortable passing by a person in need? Jesus told about a badly beaten robbery victim whom a priest and a Levite bypassed. An unlikely rescuer came on the scene—a compassionate Samaritan in contrast to the Jewish religious figures. He stopped, tended to the man's injuries, and arranged for extended care for the victim. Even in our society, in which to stop to help someone by the roadside is risky, we constantly encounter people in our paths we can help in some way by sharing our resources. We cannot simply ignore the plight of life's victims; we are called to be agents of recovery, of restoration.

A true disciple of Jesus cannot read the parable of the Rich Fool (Luke 12:13-21) without examining his or her feverish pursuit of material possessions and realizing the danger in doing so. A man had a bumper crop, made provisions to store it for his exclusive use, and assumed he had plenty; he could retire and enjoy life. He died before he could enjoy his bounty. Jesus warned that the possessions we think we control can gain mastery over our lives;

---

[9] John Claypool, *Stories Jesus Still Tells: The Parables* (Cambridge: Cowley Publications, 2000), 5.

greed can exercise tyranny over us, and we literally can spend our lives accumulating things that perish and take us with them.

Many of Jesus' stories surprise us. The parable of the Dishonest Manager (Luke 16:1-9) may puzzle us on first reading. The manager of an estate evidently had embezzled funds from his employer. An audit of the books was about to reveal the manager's theft. While time ran down, he hurriedly reduced the bills of his employer's debtors, creating IOU's he could call in when he was fired. In Jesus' story, the owner commended the dishonest manager. Did Jesus recommend dishonesty? Certainly not! He commended shrewdness, intelligence, and initiative. Jesus' followers are to be as clever in doing kingdom business as the manager was in secular wheeling and dealing.

Jesus used stories to teach by contrast. In the parable of the Persistent Widow (Luke 18:1-8), He told about a woman who kept pestering a judge until she wore him down and finally received justice. Jesus' point was not that if we pray persistently, God eventually will give in and give us what we want. Rather, if after repeated badgering a human judge reluctantly will do right, how much more and more quickly will God move to help His people?

Jesus used a devastating parable to warn against superficial religion. In the story of the Pharisee and the Tax Collector (Luke 18:9-14), He taught that realities in the spiritual realm are not as they might seem or as some might like to think. In the temple, a Pharisee's prayer reminded God how fortunate He was to have the man among God's people. The Pharisee's prayer was all about him and really was to him; it was a conversation with himself. With downcast eyes a tax collector—hated by his own people because he worked for the Romans and profited off his people—asked God for mercy. God heard his prayer and made him right. Shock waves rolled through hearers "who were confident of their own righteousness and looked down on everybody else" (v. 9). The hated tax collector left the temple justified, not the Pharisee. The man wrapped in his own religious trappings merely bolstered his smug pride; the tax collector received the mercy for which he humbly asked. Jesus won no fans among the religious leaders that day as He challenged their misguided assumptions. The story continues to warn us against the danger of allowing religious pride and arrogance to blind us to our need of God's mercy and forgiveness.

The parable of Money Management (Matt. 25:14-30) includes us all. A rich man prepared to take a trip. He gave three servants differing amounts of money to manage while he was away. Two of the servants used the money to gain more. The third servant hid his part of the money for safekeeping. When the master returned and called for an accounting, he commended and rewarded the two servants who had used his money well. He condemned the servant who had done nothing with the money left in his charge but merely had safeguarded it. The point is clear: We are to take what God has given us and are to trade with it in life's marketplace, even at risk, so God can gain return in the form of people won to Him. The parable's underlying question well may be: What are we doing with what God has given us to manage?

In the parable of the Empty House (Matt. 12:43-45), Jesus issued a chilling indictment against negative religion. A man was freed from an unclean spirit. After a time, the spirit returned to find that his former home was neat and clean but unoccupied. The unclean spirit invited seven more spirits to join him in moving into the vacant home (the man), so "the final condition of that man [was] worse than the first" (v. 45). Jesus taught that ridding oneself of bad qualities and habits and avoiding doing certain things is good and necessary but is not enough. Negatives must be replaced by positives—positive attitudes, qualities, and actions. Life rejects vacuums; it will be made up of something. People must choose wisely the contents of their lives.

In the parable of the Workers in the Vineyard (Matt. 20:1-16), Jesus told us something encouraging about God. In the story, a vineyard owner hired workers at various times in the day to harvest his grapes. When he gave the men their wages at the end of the day, even the workers hired last received a full day's pay. When the men who had worked longer complained, the owner reminded them that he had paid them the agreed wage. If he wanted to be generous with the workers hired late, what was that to the grumblers? Jesus taught that not only does God keep His end of His bargains but He also is generous beyond all expectation. God uses His supreme discretion, and He does so with love, mercy, and grace.

Of course, Jesus used many other parables to teach spiritual truths. Those that have been preserved for our study are instructional. He told many parables to teach about God's kingdom. The stories of the Buried Treasure and the Pearl of Great Price (Matt. 13:44-46) emphasize the priority and the value of entering God's kingdom. The parables of the Patch and the Wineskins and the Wine (Luke 5:36-39) stress that the old forms of religion could not contain or accommodate the new way Jesus brought. The story of the Mustard Seed (Luke 13:18-19) contrasts the kingdom's small beginning in Jesus and His disciples to its great growth. The parable of the Leaven (Luke 13:20-21) emphasizes the kingdom's active permeation of the world.

Some of Jesus' parables address people's personal responses to Him and others. The story of the Wise and Foolish Builders (Matt. 7:24-27) concludes the Sermon on the Mount and pointedly emphasizes the absolute necessity of building our lives on Jesus and His teachings. The story of the Unmerciful Servant (Matt. 18:21-35) dramatically reminds us of our great sin debt God has forgiven and of our obligation to forgive lesser sins committed against us. Matthew 25:31-46 may or may not be a parable of the final judgment using the figures of sheep and goats. If it is a parable, it is a gripping story that drives home a sobering truth: Acts such as feeding the hungry, giving water to the thirsty, offering hospitality, clothing the needy, caring for the sick, and visiting prisoners do not establish a relationship with Jesus but give solid evidence of such a relationship. Failing to perform these kinds of actions is evidence that a person is not related to Him.

The Gospels present numerous other striking stories from the most creative mind the world has known. We do well to become familiar with them, take them to heart, and put them into practice.

Jesus' parables are perfect combinations of form and substance. The appealing story form contains formidable spiritual truth. An experience from my childhood remains as a reminder that form often promises far more than it delivers. I was attending my first carnival set up in a large field behind the house in which my family lived, and the attractions and goodies captivated me. The cotton candy especially caught my eye. So much candy on a cardboard stack pole for what seemed to be so cheap a price! Imagine my surprise and disappointment when the first bite melted away to nothing but a little sugar. I had bought form without any substance.

Far from being frothy confections of a shrewd and skilled wordsmith, Jesus' parables are strong stuff. They demand reflection, assimilation, obedience, and action. Many of His stories were delivered in the crucibles of conflict but still were the appeals of love for life-changing response on the part of progressively hostile opponents.

The Parables of Lost and Found in Luke 15

We owe Luke the physician an eternal debt of gratitude. Under God's inspiration, he included the parables of Luke 15 in his Gospel. This chapter has been called "the Gospel within the Gospel."[10] The world would have suffered incalculable loss had God not inspired Luke to preserve three parables of Jesus in their volatile and emotion-charged setting during His earthly ministry.

The Lord faced increasing opposition from the Jews' religious leaders. In general, they were looking for a David-like messiah—a political/military leader who would rally his people, form a fighting force, and drive the hated Romans from the Jews' land. Some Jews anticipated a priestly messiah, but most looked for a descendant of David who would restore the nation to power and prominence. Jesus rejected that role; instead, He chose to be the Suffering Servant who would offer deliverance on a much deeper level than mere military conquest. He would offer Himself for the forgiveness of people's sins.

Jesus did not fit the prevailing expectations about the Messiah and challenged much of the religious leaders' theology—their thinking about God. They particularly were incensed that He gladly shared table fellowship with "tax collectors and 'sinners'" (Luke 15:1). The religious leaders were appalled that Jesus welcomed—received, accepted—people they deemed unacceptable.

In Jesus' day, to eat with someone was more than to extend polite hospitality; to do so was an expression of friendship. "Tax collectors" were Jews who worked for the Romans by collecting revenues and in the process grew wealthy off the heavy burden placed on their own people. The Jews hated these traitorous collaborators. Jesus called a tax collector named Levi to be His disciple (see Luke 5:27-32). Levi gave a feast at his house and invited "a large crowd of tax collectors and others" to the meal (v. 29). The Pharisees and the scribes complained bitterly to Jesus' disciples because Jesus ate "with tax collectors and 'sinners'"

---

[10] Trench, 141.

(v. 30). Evidently, on numerous occasions Jesus shared meals with people who needed His love and acceptance. "Sinners" included immoral people and people who did not keep all the minute regulations of the oral tradition that had been tacked on to the Ten Commandments.

The religious leaders' incredulous complaint arose from their abhorrence of ritual defilement and thus their careful attention to clean and unclean foods and people. Contact with Gentiles defiled a Jew. The tax collectors had constant contact with the Romans. The "sinners" ignored Judaism's food laws, thus they were ritually unclean. Jesus' eating with such people made Him ceremonially unclean. His receiving them warmly was an open declaration that He put no stock in the Jews' regulations about unclean foods and people. People were more important than religious rules.

We should be clear that Jesus' befriending tax collectors and sinners did not indicate His tolerating their wrongs. He never lessened His moral and ethical demands to win people's favor. In John 8:1-11, the Pharisees brought to Jesus a woman caught in the act of adultery. In an attempt to trap Jesus, they asked what should be done with her, for the law called for her to be stoned. When Jesus said that the man in the crowd who had no sin should cast the first stone at the woman, the gathering slowly dispersed. Jesus did not condemn the woman but sent her on her way with the admonition: "Leave your life of sin" (v. 11). The woman was to change her lifestyle, turning from immorality. Jesus offered no easy tolerance for people's sins.

In Luke 19:1-10, Jesus invited Himself to the home of a tax collector named Zacchaeus for a meal—much to the displeasure of the people who viewed the encounter. Jesus' gesture of friendship to a hated tax collector, no doubt shunned by his own people, led to a dramatic change in Zacchaeus. He declared he would give half of all he had to the poor and would more than recompense any people he had cheated. Friendship with Jesus resulted in redemptive changes in Zacchaeus. Today, people who accept Jesus' offered friendship experience the same life-changing love. Far from tolerating people's sins, Jesus offers forgiveness and a new beginning.

Jesus' eating with irreligious people whom the religious leaders felt obviously could not enjoy God's favor angered "the Pharisees and the teachers of the law" (Luke 15:2). The Pharisees were laymen dedicated to keeping the Law and the long list of rules in the oral tradition that had developed around the Ten Commandments, which they viewed as being as sacred as the Commandments. The teachers of the law were scribes who first copied the Hebrew Scriptures and then grew to be experts who interpreted and taught the law. These rigid legalists had no room in their theology or their relationships for people who, in their view, were not as religious as they were. In their view, to rub shoulders with irreligious people was to become contaminated. They felt strongly that no self-respecting teacher who expected Judaism's stamp of approval could accept the nobodies and outcasts of His society as Jesus did.

Jesus not only offered His friendship to the social and religious rejects of His society, but He also offered His friendship to the religious leaders; He extended to them acceptance as He did to the tax collectors and sinners. He was an equal-opportunity guest. On various occasions, He ate with religious leaders. In response to a Pharisee's invitation, Jesus went to his home and shared a meal with him (Luke 7:36). In Luke 11:37, another Pharisee invited Jesus to a meal in his house, and Jesus again accepted. In both instances, Jesus was criticized rather than being treated well as a guest. Again, in Luke 14:1, Jesus went to a Pharisee's home to eat with the man. The people present watched Jesus carefully and tested Him—in our vernacular, He was set up. So instead of allowing Jesus' presence and His offer of acceptance to bring warmth, joy, and God's transforming grace to their lives, most of the religious leaders hardened themselves in their opposition to Jesus and heightened their resolve to do away with Him.

In answer to the complaint (actually, the charge) that Jesus—and by implication, God, for whom He insisted He spoke and acted—accepted and befriended the dregs of Jewish society as people of worth, Jesus told three parables. He did so to defend His willingness to receive all people, no matter what their conditions or stations in life. In a context charged with hostility, Jesus answered His critics. He refused to be intimidated and to back down from His mission to offer God's grace and love to people in all strata of life. Throughout His brief earthly ministry, He extended open acceptance to everyone He encountered.

The story of the shepherd who had 100 sheep and went in search of the one sheep who was lost (Luke 15:3-7) appears in Matthew

18:12-14 in a different context. (Jesus well may have repeated parables in various teaching situations.) In both instances, Jesus emphasized the importance of each person to God. In both, He argued from the lesser to the greater. If one sheep was so valuable to a shepherd, how much more valuable is each person to God?

Among the Gospel writers, only Luke included the parable of the lost coin (Luke 15:8-10). The story's point is that if one lost coin out of ten was important to a woman, how much more important is every individual to God? Both the parable of the shepherd and his one lost sheep and the story of the woman and her lost coin stress the diligence of the people's searches for what was lost. Jesus sounded and sustained a new note in the religious context of His day: God comes in search of each person who is separated from Him. He wants to bring everyone to Himself and takes the initiative to do so.

The Consummate Parable

The third parable in Luke 15 is unique to Luke's Gospel. It is the apex of Jesus' defense of His ministry in the face of the religious leaders' criticism and bitter complaint. More than that, I consider it to be the greatest, most thought-provoking of all Jesus' parables.

Some interpreters have pointed out the movement in Jesus' three parables in Luke 15 from one lost sheep out of one hundred to one lost coin out of ten to one lost son out of two. This approach views the numbers as a device Jesus used to heighten the third parable's intensity. In reality, however, the third parable's intensity is heightened even more, for the third story involves two lost sons. As the story unfolds, Jesus made evident that the older brother who stayed at home was as lost to the father in a far country of attitude as the younger son had been in the geographical far country.

Prominent figures in early church history produced commentaries on the parable in Luke 15:11-32. Tertullian, Clement of Alexandria, Gregory Thaumaturgus, Ambrose, Jerome, and Augustine offered interpretations of the parable. In addition, "it has lent itself as a subject for great painters (Durer, Behan, Rembrandt, L. Bassano, G. van Honthorst), dramatists (Tudor Dramatists, Gascoigne's *Glasse of Government*), choreographers

(Balanchine), musicians (Animuccia, Prokofiev, Britten), litterateurs (A. Gide, *L'Enfant prodigal*) and philosophers (Nietzsche)."[11]

Luke 15:11-32 has been called the greatest short story ever told. It has been given various titles. Traditionally it has been called the Parable of the Prodigal Son. English Bibles of the sixteenth century gave this title in marginal notes. Possibly, this inclusion reflected a similar title in the Latin Vulgate. Jesus' story also has been called the Parable of the Lost Son, the Parable of the Waiting Father, the Parable of Two Lost Sons, and the Parable of the Loving Father. As a title, I prefer the Parable of the Compassionate Father, for the father is the central figure in the story, and the emphasis is on his compassion for both his sons. Jesus' story is about God's inclusive love and compassion that reach out to all people—people who are trying to earn a relationship with God through keeping religious rules and individuals who despair of God's accepting them because they feel they are so grossly sinful He cannot love them. Jesus' story of a father's stubborn, persistent love for his two sons forever will be a clear, challenging, and encouraging insight into God's character, an open invitation for all people to accept His love and forgiveness, and a warning about people's relationships with Him and with one another.

Someone may object that Jesus' story is not about reclaiming sinners—both irreligious and religious—because the boys in the parable were already members of the father's family. Thus, the story must be about "backslidden" believers. I contend that although both boys were their father's offspring, neither was a son in the highest, truest, and intended sense. In Acts 17:28, Paul quoted pagan poets who declared that people are God's "offspring." He is Creator, and all people are His creatures. Yet to become His children with a redemptive relationship with Him, individuals must repent and place their faith in Christ. Only then do people become "heirs of God and co-heirs with Christ" (Rom. 8:17).

As was pointed out earlier, most often Jesus' parables have one main point. They are not allegories in the strict sense—stories in which each detail has symbolic meaning. Considering Jesus' stories

---

[11] Joseph A. Fitzmyer, "The Gospel According to Luke X–XXIV," vol. 28a in *The Anchor Bible* (Garden City, New York: Doubleday & Company, Inc., 1985), 1083.

The Compassionate Father

to be allegories has produced some wild, improbable, and even humorous interpretations. Some of His parables, however, have allegorical or symbolic elements. In Luke 15:11-32, the father clearly represents God; the younger son represents the tax collectors and sinners who were drawn to Jesus and received His acceptance; and the elder brother represents the Jews' religious leaders. Beyond this clear symbolism, to see every element in the story as having hidden meaning runs the risk of distorting Jesus' intention for the story.

Tertullian, an early church father, offered an allegorical interpretation of the parable in Luke 15:11-32. "The Elder Son in the story is the Jew; the Younger, the Christian. The patrimony of which the Younger claimed his share is that knowledge of God which a man has by his birthright. The citizen in the far country to whom he hired himself is the devil. The robe bestowed on the returning prodigal is that sonship which Adam lost at the Fall; the ring is the sign and seal of baptism; the feast is the Lord's Supper. And who is 'the fatted calf', slain for the feast, but the Saviour (sic) himself?"[12] Such allegorizing distorts the parables, twisting them into unrecognizable shapes. The major thrust of the parable in Luke 15:11-32 is God's love and compassion for all people.

Where did Jesus get His material for His stories? I do not believe He created His parables on the spur of the moment. He could have done so, but I feel that He observed people, took note of their experiences, pondered what He saw and heard, and stored the information away for the exact moment or moments He could use it with maximum impact to impart a needed revelation of truth from and about God. Jesus was a keen observer of the world around Him and selected elements of that world to use in His teachings. I easily can believe that the incident of the shepherd who went in search of one sheep outside his fold took place around Nazareth. Jesus' inspired ingenuity made the comparison with God's seeking people outside His enfolding love and stored the event away to be retrieved at the most advantageous moment or moments. Jesus used the incident to reveal a striking new truth that was foreign to the religious leaders of His day: God does not wait until people are religiously correct or good before He will accept

---

[12] Hunter, *Interpreting the Parables*, 24.

them. He takes the initiative to bring people into the fold of His grace.

In like manner, the incident of the woman who searched until she found her lost coin well could have been widely known in Nazareth. It emphasized to Jesus that God makes every effort to retrieve people lost to Him. In the celebrations following the shepherd's and the woman's successful searches, Jesus expressed vividly the unbounded pleasure God experiences when people are recovered from being lost to Him.

Jesus well could have been familiar with an incident reflected in the story of the compassionate father and his two sons. Perhaps the account of an actual father's dealings with his sons was well known in the area around Nazareth during Jesus' years there. Did Jesus know the family? Did He have contact with the boys involved? Of course, we only can speculate. Yet the story is so rich in details centered in real life that I cannot escape the feeling it was part of the tapestry of life in and around Nazareth when Jesus was there.

Jesus' story in Luke 15:11-32 has fascinated Bible students for centuries, probably from the time it was transmitted orally. Archibald M. Hunter called it "the pearl among the parables."[13] Robert Bridges declared it to be "a perfectly flawless piece of work."[14] Others have considered it to be the greatest of Jesus' parables and the most magnificent short story ever told. That it is a short story with a compact story line and an unexpected ending—actually, with no ending—highlights Jesus' ingenuity and matchless artistry in storytelling.

I like books of short stories. I can read a complete story in a brief time, unlike tackling some of the tomes for which the writers obviously got paid by the word or the page. Good short story writers present spellbinding plots, intense action, and surprise endings that entertain readers and leave them with a sense of satisfaction or cause them to continue reflecting on the stories. Jesus' third parable in Luke 15 can be read in a few minutes, but it offers material for almost endless meditation in an effort to apply its truths to life.

---

[13] Archibald M. Hunter, *The Parables Then and Now* (Philadelphia: The Westminster Press, 1971), 59.
[14] Ibid, 59.

Jesus' short story in Luke 15:11-32 has all the elements of a magnificent presentation. Joseph A. Fitzmyer, quoting G. V. Jones, pointed out that the parable "combines into a succinct pattern such themes as Freedom and Responsibility, Estrangement, the Personalness of Life, Longing and Return, Grace, Anguish, and Reconciliation . . . universal characteristics of life and . . . basic human needs."[15]

In spite of many reverent and insightful attempts to explore Jesus' probing parable, no one has been able to plumb the story's depths fully. Each reading provokes a new thought, reveals a new truth, or issues a new challenge. Countless sermons, Bible lessons, and books have not been able to exhaust the implications of Jesus' words. In the light of this truth, I approach the parable with no illusions of finding what no one else has found, of mining previously undiscovered gold. Out of my great appreciation for the sheer genius of a story Jesus left open-ended, I want to explore its meaning for me, for people who have received God's amazing and incomprehensible love, and for others outside God's kingdom by choice to whom God goes on offering His inclusive grace and for whom He has measureless compassion.

A Mural of Rich Colors

My approach to the greatest unfinished short story ever told will be along the lines of an actual event rather than of a once-upon-a-time story from imagination—even divine imagination. I see it as a drama from real life.

To switch metaphors, to me Jesus' unfinished story is a mural with various scenes, shapes, and shades—a word painting with vivid colors and rich hues. A mural is a painting on a wall or a ceiling. The painting may be large, or it may consist of successive scenes extending over a lengthy area. I like to think of Jesus' story in Luke 15:11-32 as a series of scenes in lifelike colors. As the Master Artist, He drew from His extensive palette of words and images to produce an unforgettable mural that forces us to look at ourselves honestly.

Every so often, I watch a television program on the Public Television Network that presents an artist who begins with a blank canvas and in an hour produces a breathtaking painting. I

---

[15] Fitzmyer, 1084.

understand that the artist is dead and that the series continues from programs taped in past years. I have no artistic ability, and I am fascinated as I watch the artist begin the painting. Step by step, he explains what he is doing, the brushes he is using, the paints on his palate, and the combinations of colors he employs. I watch while the painting takes shape. At points when I think the painting is complete, the artist adds touches that result in an amazing scene of startling beauty. Jesus' artistry with words in Luke 15:11-32 created an infinitely more astonishing, important, and enduring work of beauty.

Several years ago, my wife and I had the privilege of accompanying my daughter, son-in-law, and granddaughter to London and Paris. While we were in Paris, we visited the Louvre. I somewhat impatiently waited my turn to get a front-row look at the Mona Lisa. When I finally stepped to the front and stood before that famous painting, I had a feeling of awe and reverence as I realized I was viewing one of the great art masterpieces of all time. I marveled at Leonardo da Vinci's great skill. Yet my response to the painting and the painter pales in comparison with my continuing fascination with the Master Storyteller's wondrous word picture in Luke 15:11-32. Leonardo da Vinci was an exceptionally talented human who produced a one-of-a-kind, priceless painting. Jesus was God in human flesh who gave us a clear look into the Father's loving, compassionate heart and who forced us to look searchingly at ourselves.

Jesus painted an incomparable, riveting mural with words. That matchless painting with successive scenes continues to impact the lives of all people who study it seriously. As we look closely at the mural, we will see our faces in the crowd. Look for yourself as you view the wide scope of the mural. I have found myself in more than one scene. Perhaps you will, also. Stand with me before the first scene.

Scene 1: A Hasty Departure (vv. 11-13)

11 *Jesus continued: "There was a man who had two sons.* **12** *The younger one said to his father, 'Father, give me my share of the estate.' So he divided his property between them.*
13 *Not long after that, the younger son got together all he had, set off for a distant country and there squandered his wealth in wild living."*

Jesus had told two brief revelation-laden stories about people who searched for and found lost items—a lost animal and a lost coin. Then, in quick succession, He related the third dramatic and longer short story I feel was drawn from real life. Jesus began rather abruptly: "There was a man who had two sons" (v. 11). The father was doubly blessed. A primary goal of every male Jew was to sire a son who would extend the family line. A man who fathered multiple sons was viewed as highly blessed. The psalmist had written, "Like arrows in the hand of a warrior are sons born in one's youth. Blessed is the man whose quiver is full of them" (Ps. 127:4-5a). The two sons in Jesus' story would share in family labor, provide assistance in the parents' old age, and ensure the parents' immortality by continuing the family line. Jesus did not mention a mother or daughters, who probably made up the family unit. The father and his two sons were most germane to His story.

Literally, Jesus referred to "a certain man" (Greek text). If names would have meant anything to His audience, could Jesus have supplied them? Could He have begun, "Ezra had two sons, Joshua the younger and Caleb the older"? Perhaps. Jesus' approach, however, made an important point at the outset: The father in the story had *two* sons. This early emphasis perfectly sets the theme and tenor of what follows. The story has three main characters: the father, the younger son, and the older son. The parable is about all three, not merely about the father and the younger or prodigal son. The central figure is the father as he related to both his sons. I think Jesus' primary objective in His story was to convey to tax collectors, sinners, and religious leaders the good news about God's gracious disposition toward all people—self-styled good people proud of their righteousness and sure of their standing with God, and individuals whose lives were marked by obvious sins. The former individuals were self-deceived; the latter well may have wondered whether God could love or accept them, if He regarded them at all.

As was His insightful practice, Jesus used the familiar family setting for His story. Appropriate for that day, the father in Jesus' story was the prominent figure. Doubtless, a wife and mother stood in the background and remained there—also appropriate for the customs of that time. The father likely was a wealthy landowner. Information later in the parable indicates that he had hired laborers (*misthioi*, v. 17) and slaves (*doulous*, v. 22), although he and his sons likely worked the land also, in the form of manual labor and/or supervision. In a later scene, the father had the means to provide a lavish banquet for everyone connected with the farm and to hire entertainers for a festive celebration (vv. 24-25). Evidently, he was a man of considerable resources.

Beyond all doubt, the father in Jesus' story represents God. Jesus used the figure of an incisive, wise, sensitive, and caring human father to present timeless insights into God's character. At the outset of His story, Jesus expressed a startling truth about God: God can be described best as Father in the highest and healthiest sense of that word. Tragically, to some people today, the word *father* evokes painful memories and emotions. They had (or have) abusive, insensitive, unloving, overbearingly controlling, indifferent, or absentee fathers. To call God *Father,* however, is to attribute to Him perfect, ideal fatherhood. He is the Father who loves us, provides for us, listens to us, comforts us, shares our pain, and affirms and encourages us. His care for us never falters.

The Old Testament contains references to God as Israel's Shepherd (see Isa. 40:11; Ezek. 34:1-12). In Psalm 95:6-7, the writer declared: "Come, let us bow down in worship, let us kneel before the Lord our Maker; for he is our God and we are the people of his pasture, the flock under his care." David made a significant advance on that concept when he called God his personal Shepherd in Psalm 23:1: "The Lord is *my* shepherd" (italics mine). The writer of Psalm 103 imparted heightened revelation when he compared God's attitude toward His faithful people with a father's tender care: "As a father has compassion on his children, so the Lord has compassion on them who fear him" (Ps. 103:13). Jesus extended that concept further when He taught His disciples to address God as their personal "Father" (Matt. 6:9). In Luke 15:11-32, Jesus portrayed God as the compassionate Father who loves all people and seeks to include them as His children.

Jesus' story in Luke 15:11-32 reflects the age-old axiom that youth will be served. Often, the young are impatient to try their wings. In their thinking, they are meant to soar with eagles, not to be grounded among turkeys! As a popular song of another time expressed, each has a secret pair of wings and longs to fly. Such yearning is not inherently wrong if it is accompanied by patient preparation and proper timing. After all, what young boy has not dreamed of and longed for independence from parental control? Many youngsters have chaffed at what they perceived to be restraints that denied them what they defined as freedom: license to pursue whatever they wanted. Helmut Thielicke wrote: "The son [in Jesus' story] has a dreadful fear that he will not taste life to the full, that he may miss something."[1]

Of course, such anxious and oftentimes frantic pursuit of the good life—all of what a person perceives to be the best things life should offer—is not limited to the young. Adults of all ages succumb to the siren song of the full life waiting on the other side of the next rise in the road. Out there somewhere is unbridled happiness. How many adults are engaged in a feverish chase after things and experiences that will eliminate the uneasy feeling life is passing them by? They are plagued by the haunting feeling that what they have and where they are in life pale in comparison with what is out there that others are enjoying. Their self-imposed crisis does not occur solely in mid-life but at any point in the long stretch of adulthood when dissatisfaction gives rise to immature, reckless decisions and actions.

In the brevity of Jesus' story, the younger son's request is introduced abruptly. In the life setting, my guess is the son probably worked up his nerve over a period of time. Perhaps in his growing frustration at his unsatisfying life on the farm, he gradually summoned up courage to approach his father. To me, Jesus' brevity in His story's beginning probably does not express the son's impulsiveness so much as it telescopes a fairly lengthy process. He had been thinking about his unsatisfactory situation for a long time. At some point, when he could wait no longer, the younger son in Jesus' story asked for his portion of what eventually would be his. He said: "Give me my share of the estate"—literally, "the part of the substance falling to me" (v. 12, Greek text). He wanted his father to divide the father's possessions or property and to give him his share of the inheritance to which he was entitled and which would be his at the father's death.

Many readers have interpreted the young man's request as an insult to his father. They have viewed the request as indicating the son's wish that his father was dead so the son could receive his part

---

[1] Helmut Thielicke, *The Waiting Father* (New York: Harper & Row, Publishers, 1959), 20.

of the estate. To me, the insult did not lie there. The son's words did indicate a rather callous attitude toward his father—a lack of concern for his father's feelings. In Jesus' day, however, a father could divide the inheritance while he lived. This sometimes occurred. When the father in Jesus' story did so, the older son received two-thirds of the estate. If the father had daughters, their dowries would have been provided out of the older son's two-thirds share. The younger son received one-third of the father's possessions. Even when the father divided the inheritance, he was entitled to live off the proceeds of the estate until his death.

To me, the younger son's request to his father expressed the young man's desire for his idealized and unrealistic concept of freedom. Insult in the son's request was at the point of impetuously asking for his part of the inheritance instead of waiting for the father to offer to divide the estate while he still lived. Evidently, the son had no thought of how his request would affect his father. He thought only of himself.

The request also reflected the young man's woefully inadequate view of sonship—of his relationship with his father. To him, life on the farm was filled with constraints that stifled him. He viewed his father's directives as confining, controlling, and sometimes unreasonable.

The younger son also had to live with a rigid, workaholic older brother. Work on the farm was daily drudgery to which the younger son saw no end and from which he derived no fulfillment. For him, one dreary, boring, tiring day followed another in monotonous succession. How could he find himself in such an environment? He was meant for bigger and better things. Surely life was meant to be made up of much more than what he presently was experiencing. Somewhere people were enjoying wine, music, dancing, and laughter. His life had empty places he wanted to fill with entertainment and amusement.

The younger son wanted the freedom to experience life's pleasures—to explore and to experiment. To do so, he needed to finance the lifestyle for which he longed. He did it in the only way open to him. He presumptuously asked his father for what eventually would come to him anyway. He could not wait another day; he was suffocating in the farm's bland, uninspiring, demanding confines. He was impatient to get on with life as he wanted it to be and dreamed it could be. His request was his first downward step to a state that later would be described by the words "dead" and "lost" (vv. 24, 32).

Reflected in the younger son's bold, rash request was his focus on himself: "Give *me my* share of the estate" (v. 12, italics mine). He and his dreams of the good life comprised the center of his world. He had little or no thought of other family members and of the emotional pain he was causing them. Surely, in the background, a mother agonized over her son's decision. The patriarchal culture of Jesus' day is reflected in His focus on the father in the family. In fact, the young man was brushing aside God's Commandment to honor his parents—not simply to obey them but to take care of them when they no longer could fend for themselves. He would leave that to his stuffy older brother, who was content to work the family farm. Immature, headstrong, and self-absorbed, the young man was bent on escaping from a dull, drab, intolerable existence and on making an exciting dash to a life of ease, enjoyment, excitement, and adventure.

In the economy of Jesus' story, He simply said, "And the one [the father] divided to them the goods [life]" (v. 12, literal translation). The father honored his younger son's request. Note the plural "them." The older son also received his share of the estate: two-thirds of the material goods.

What went on between the younger son's request and the division of the estate? I imagine the father sat down with his impetuous son and tried to reason with him. The father's love, expressed so eloquently later in the story, would not have let the son go easily. A mother's love spilled over in tears that accompanied prayers for her son. We are not told how old the sons were, but that they evidently were not married points to relatively young ages. Perhaps the younger son was past his mid-teens; the older son may have been nearing 20. Normally the marriageable age for Jewish males was between 18 and 20 years of age. At any rate, the father was aware of his younger son's immaturity. The son wanted to explore the vast, exciting world beyond the farm, but he had no idea of what awaited him: the temptations, threats, and dangers that masqueraded as good times. The father knew a lot about what his son would encounter, and no doubt he wanted to protect the boy from himself.

If the younger son was anything like young people today and in every generation, he insisted he knew what he were doing.

Whatever came, he could handle it. He was ready to be his own man, to go his own way, to chart his own course and claim his destiny. John Claypool wrote, "This young man had not done his homework: he did not know himself or the world."[2] Seeing that the son was determined to break away, the father granted his request.

As soon as he could (literally, "not many days after"), the younger son "got together all he had" (v. 13). In the Greek text, the phrase is "having gathered together all things." The words actually convey the idea of converting everything to cash. The young man could not wait to enjoy his freedom to do as he pleased. Likely, the father bought the one-third interest in the estate out of the two-thirds remaining for the older brother. Normally, among the Jews every effort was made to keep property in the family. If this occurred, technically the older brother then owned everything; at his father's death, he would inherit the entire estate. The father later would state as much in verse 31.

The younger son had the money he needed to finance his freedom, so he "set off"—literally, he "went on travel." The Greek word can mean "to be absent from home or country." The younger son quickly left home. The lone Greek term for leaving home is poignant. Converting everything to cash and leaving home meant the younger son was burning his bridges behind him. He was severing ties with home. He left nothing that would draw him back. Literally and figuratively, he turned his back on his father and home. He never meant to come back home; if he ever did return, he would do so on his terms—with all the trappings of success to show he had managed quite well on his own. Someday, he might visit the old homestead and the homefolk—riding on a fine animal, dressed in the finest robe, and wearing rings on his fingers to show his family how far he had risen in the world.

Some interpreters have criticized the father for letting his son leave. They have contended that such a father could not represent God because He is not an indulgent Father who dotes on His children to their detriment, letting them do as they please to their hurt. Of course, the father in Jesus' story could have denied the son's request; then the son would have had no resources for independent living. He would have had to stay home. Yet in a real

---

[2] John R. Claypool, *The Saga of Life: Living Gracefully though All of the Stages* (New Orleans: Insight Press, 2003), 56.

The Compassionate Father

sense, to force the son to stay would have meant that the father would have lost him as a son. The son would have been at home physically, but he would have been bitter, angry, and resentful. He would have been home in body only. His heart would have been in the far, bright country of his imagining. He would have been alienated in attitude and emotions. Likely, no relationship of love would have existed. Perhaps only the hard lessons of life would help the son recognize and appreciate the true value of sonship, a father's love, and the security and warmth of home and family. Maybe the only way the father could hope to have the young man as a true son was to let the boy come to his moment of truth on his own. The young man would have to *want* to be home in order really to *be* at home.

What a gut-wrenching experience the son's departure must have been for the father—and in the background, for a weeping mother! As they watched his slowly diminishing figure in the distance, emotions beyond expression must have churned in both of them. A child's leaving home—in positive circumstances or in negative ones—always has been and still is charged with gut-wrenching emotions. Today, whether a child angrily leaves home, goes away to college, moves to another city for employment, joins the military, or is deployed to another country for active military duty, parents' emotions are stirred deeply. A child's running away with no indication of destination and little if any means of subsistence constitutes a major crisis for any family. In Jesus' story, although the son had adequate resources, his naïve confidence that he had things well in hand was alarming. The father must have been moved beyond description by his son's decision to leave home and his quick, decisive action in doing so. The son's undisguised eagerness to distance himself from his father added further insult to unthinking and uncaring injury.

At the beginning of His story, Jesus taught a significant lesson about God. The younger son's father did not force him to stay home. The emphatic point is that love does not coerce. It invites, appeals, and reasons; but it does not force itself on another. To me, the most incredible statements in the Scriptures are in 1 John 4:8,16: "God is love." The chief mark of His character, the essence of His nature, is love—sacrificial, self-giving good will that has others' best interests at heart and is offered repeatedly even when its objects reject it. God's love is unmotivated; that is, it has no tinge of "what's in it for Me." He does not offer it on the basis of merit but simply because a person *is* and needs His love. Every person needs God's transforming, assuring, and sustaining love, and He extends it to everyone.

I am convinced John's amazing, inspired insight that God is love came from his observing Jesus' life and ministry in which He consistently demonstrated God's kind of love. I also wonder whether the insight additionally came from Jesus' teachings—and more specifically, the revealing parable in Luke 15:11-32. Because it is preserved in the Scriptures, the story made a deep impression on the hearers. Did the apostle John retain in memory Jesus' thought-provoking story long after the Lord was no longer present physically? If so, John's inspired statement is graphic testimony to the staying power of Jesus' remarkable parable.

Theologians have used the terms *omniscient, omnipotent,* and *omnipresent* to describe God. Yet what would all knowledge, all power, and universal presence mean apart from love? All knowledge without love would be cold, detached intellect. All power without love would be brute force. Universal presence without love would be nerve-racking threat and intimidation. The father in Jesus' story loved his son enough that he would not use leverage to force his son to do what the father knew was best for his boy.

The younger son sinned against his father's love. He turned his back on the person who truly cared for him. Malcolm O. Tolbert wrote: "The story shows that man's love is narrow, shortsighted, contingent, selfish. On the other hand, God's love is boundless, profound, reconciling, unreserved."[3] The son's quick departure and the manner in which he left was a declaration that in his mind he neither needed nor valued his father's love.

Jesus' word picture of the younger son's willful and perhaps somewhat rudely leaving home, bent on putting distance between his father and him, underscores vividly the seriousness of people's sin. We can commit no greater sin than to sin against God's love for us. The suggestion that many of us have difficulty really grasping the great truth that God really does love us, just as we are with weaknesses and flaws, is doubtless accurate. Yet the Scriptures

---

[3] Malcolm O. Tolbert, "Luke" in *The Broadman Bible Commentary*, vol. 9 (Nashville: Broadman Press, 1970), 125.

reiterate the glad news that God loves each of us in spite of our sins—and even when we cannot or will not love ourselves. Jesus' atoning death on our behalf forever declares God's unwavering and undying love for us. When we throw that clearly demonstrated love back in His face, we do much more than insult Him; we sin against His love and inflict indescribable pain on Him. Turning away from God is no light matter. We do well to consider the implications of doing so.

I have been intrigued with Jesus' use of the concept of home and the word *house* to symbolize God's presence. In Jesus' story, the son's leaving home symbolized people's moving away from God; coming home would be returning to their real and intended home. Home truly is where the heart is, and the heart really is a lonely, restless nomad until it is at home with God. Interestingly, in John 14:2 Jesus referred to heaven as His father's "house," which has "many rooms." The father's house presents images of warmth, love, security, provision, and joy. In his pursuit of freedom, the younger son in Jesus' story failed to recognize that he already enjoyed true freedom—the freedom of being his father's son and of growing toward maturity in his father's guidance and care.

I am convinced that the father in Jesus' story had no desire to keep his sons under his control and dependent on him in a negative way. He wanted them to develop into mature, responsible adults who made wise choices and moved toward realizing their potential. To be sure, they were dependent on him for their livelihood, and no doubt he was glad to provide for them. Yet nothing in the account indicates he wanted to keep them under his thumb out of a need to control them.

Today, parents who keep children dependent are seeking to fill a need the parents have—a need to control, to feel needed, to be seen as superior in the sense of always knowing what is best for children, and perhaps even to realize unfulfilled dreams through them. Dependent children become struggling adults who are products of unhealthy parenting. Insightful, mature parents seek to equip children to be independent—to reach the point where the children can leave the nest to make good, responsible decisions and to shape their own lives in a healthy manner in the confidence that the parents continue to love, support, and encourage them. Everything in Jesus' story points to a wise, caring, and insightful father who wanted the best for both his sons.

The younger son traveled to "a distant country" (v. 13). Jesus did not identify the country. Suggestions include the Decapolis, 10 predominantly Gentile cities on the eastern side of the Jordan River; Alexandria in Egypt; and Rome. The place may have been one of these or none of them. The exact area is not important. The key word in the Greek text is "distant." The young man wanted to get as far away from home as possible so he would have no interference from family members; out from under his parents' watchful eyes, he could do as he pleased. As fast as he could, he traveled as far as he could from home. With illusion fueled by fantasy, He made his getaway.

The "distant country" was confirmed outwardly by geographical location, but the younger son already had reached it inwardly by attitude. The more dissatisfied, resentful, and self-centered he became, the more he neared the far country of self-detachment from a love that wanted only the best for him—from a father who loved him for who he was and what he could become, not for what he had or what he could do for his father. When we question God's unmotivated love and constant care for us, we move into the far country of ultimate distrust. When we treasure *bios* (life) in the sense of things rather than *zoe* (life God gives in relation to Him), we move into the far country where we stake everything on what is temporary and passing. Not only that, but we are reduced to self-reliance—a scary circumstance in which we set life in a downward slide in which we depend on our own limited resources. The danger is that deep within we can be moving to far countries whose distance from the Father is not measured in miles.

The younger son's first step toward ruin was his request to his father for the son's share of the inheritance. The second step was the younger son's turning his back on his father and home and insisting on going his own way.

One suggested definition of sin is to doubt that God has our best interests at heart. Sin entered the stream of human history when Adam and Eve doubted that God was being honest with them (see Gen. 3). He drew boundaries for their own good; doubt questioned whether He was holding out on them, keeping from them pleasures that would enrich their lives. Doubt led to mistrust. Reflected in the younger son's actions in Jesus' parable was the conviction that life with his father was lived in the shadow of prison walls or chain-link fences. To that young man, real life was defined in terms of no boundaries, no walls, no fences, and no interferences. In a real sense, in his mind his father stood between him and the good life.

Also implied in the young man's request and actions was his conviction that he knew what was best for him and was determined to seize his destiny on his terms, apart from his father. He did not need anyone to dictate the direction of his life. He could make his decisions without his father's help, and he could fend nicely for himself. The scene in Luke 15:11-13 is an eerie reflection of Genesis 3. In that account of the human journey's early days, Adam and Eve decided they would call the shots in their lives; they would take control and determine their destinies. And they did! They assumed the driver's seat, and immediately the vehicle of their lives careened out of control. Human history began its downward slide that has continued to the alarming carnage of our time. To say to God, "Give me the keys; I'll drive," is to invite disaster. If we insist, He will honor our request, but we will be responsible for the wreckage.

I recall an incident that continues to serve as a real-life parable for me. When I was a young boy, my parents and I often visited an aunt and uncle, who lived a few miles outside of town on a farm. On one occasion, the oldest of my three girl cousins asked her mother for the keys to the family's truck so she and her two sisters could go for a drive. My aunt tried to talk her out of going because the daughter was not an experienced driver. The daughter insisted. My aunt finally relented, and the three cousins drove away. A short time later, someone stopped at the farm to report the daughters had been in a wreck a few miles down the road. The truck had run off the road and into a creek. Fortunately, the girls were not hurt badly, but they had caused a great deal of damage, some of it in the forms of anxiety and alarmed concern. Hopefully, they learned a lesson the hard way.

Of course, as with any analogy, the real-life illustration breaks down if it is pressed. We do not cajole God into giving us our way. We do not wear Him down until He relents. To me, my cousins' experience serves as a lesson about willful immaturity that insists on its own way—often with disastrous results. On a spiritual level, God gives us the freedom to insist on our choices.

The younger son in Jesus' story insisted on his own way. His actions reveal self-will, self-assertion, and self-absorption. As in the case of Adam and Eve in Genesis 3, the younger son's story is the story of us all. None of us is a stranger to a wrong-headed, stubborn insistence on what we want.

In Jesus' parable, the intoxication of good times dulled any ambition the younger son had to become successful by building on his inheritance. In the distant country, he "squandered his wealth in wild living"—literally, "he wasted his substance by living unsavingly" (v. 13). This was his third step down the path to disaster. The young man ran through his funds quickly. In reality, his resources came from his father; his wealth had come from his father's graciously granting his request. The young man's handling of his possessions not only revealed immaturity and a decided lack of wisdom but also expressed ingratitude.

The Greek word translated "squandered" is interesting and suggestive. It is the opposite of the phrase "got [gathered] together" earlier in verse 13. The term rendered "squandered" literally means "to scatter" and was used to describe the process of winnowing grain. In Jesus' time, people threshed grain by beating the stalks with sticks, using animals to trample the stalks, or using sleds or sledges to separate the grain from the stalks. The threshing floor was in an open place exposed to wind. Late in the day, workers would use forks and then shovels to throw the grain and stalks into the air. The wind would blow the stalks and chaff away, allowing the grain to fall at the workers' feet. The young man in Jesus' story literally threw his money away.

The image of the threshing floor is foreign to me. I have never observed the process, so all I know is what I have read about it. Yet we all are acquainted with wind's sometimes powerful effects. An experience from boyhood involving wind's force makes Jesus' image come alive for me. In back of the big, white, frame house in which I grew up was a large open field. It once had been a vast yard for drying lumber produced in a huge mill that flourished at the beginning of the twentieth century. I sometimes flew kites in that field, and I recall losing one when the kite reached a height where a strong wind pulled the string from my hands and swept the kite away. I remember standing helplessly as I watched the kite slowly diminish in the distance until it disappeared from sight. Although I did not purposely lose it, I failed to gauge correctly the force of the wind, and I tried to fly the kite too high. My errors in judgment and lack of foresight cost me in terms of time, energy, and materials. The wind carried the kite away, beyond my

The Compassionate Father

reclaiming it. No doubt, the younger son did not consciously decide to throw his wealth away. He made a series of bad decisions that cost him.

A colloquialism I often heard in my small Mississippi hometown to describe someone's wasting money or opportunity was: "He (or she) threw it to the wind." The saying creates the mental image of something's being swept swiftly away, forever beyond reclaiming. The words aptly describe what the young man in Jesus' story did. He scattered to the wind the bits and pieces of his wealth.

Another common phrase for waste I heard during my childhood years was that someone had "frittered away" time, opportunity, or money. It was apparent to me that the phrase meant someone had lost something through carelessness. Imagine my surprise when I discovered that the verb *fritter* is not a word coined by southerners but actually is in the dictionary! The word means "to waste (energy, time, money, etc.) bit by bit on trifling or petty things."[4] A rare meaning is "to break, cut, or tear into small pieces."[5] In Jesus' story, the younger son diminished his funds coin by coin, bit by bit.

The Greek term Jesus used to describe the young man's lifestyle—translated "unsavingly"—can have the sense of failing to save, of spending extravagantly, and of living recklessly. J. B. Phillips translated verse 13b, "He squandered his wealth in the wildest extravagance."[6] Clarence Jordan rendered the statement: "He threw his money away living like a fool."[7] Because the term can have the sense of debauchery, profligacy, some interpreters see in the term the idea of wild and sinful living, giving credence to the older brother's later charge that the younger son wasted the father's money "with prostitutes" (v. 30). From this meaning comes the term *prodigal*, which came to be used of the young man and, in my mind, as an unfortunate title of Jesus' entire parable.

My father had a saying I heard him use numbers of times as I was growing up. When he or someone else made a rash, foolish choice or acted unwisely, my dad would say that he or another person had

---

[4] *Webster's New World Dictionary of the English Language: College Edition* (Cleveland: The World Publishing Company 1964), 581.
[5] Ibid.
[6] J. B. Phillips, *The Gospels in Modern English* (New York: The McMillan Company, 1954), 159.
[7] Clarence Jordan, *The Cotton Patch Version of Luke and Acts* (New York: Association Press, 1969), 62.

"played the wild." The phrase did not necessarily mean the person lived immorally or wickedly. Rather, instead of deliberating carefully, the individual had made a hasty, careless, and oftentimes costly mistake.

What contributed to the young man's careless handling of his money and his throwing off all restraints in the distant land? His actions are a familiar story to far too many parents today. Some children freed from parental oversight revel in their freedom to the point of discarding healthy guidelines and standards. The younger son had viewed his father's guidelines as repressive—restraints that squeezed enjoyment out of life, leaving only the withered rind of reluctant duty. Now he was free! He could do anything he wanted instead of having to please others. In hostile reaction to parental authority, he lived to please himself.

Who of us does not recall the exhilaration of beginning to make decisions without parental input? I remember how I felt when I began moving from parental control to a measure of freedom, first in college and later in seminary. Although I did not rebel in hostility, I frequently felt a kind of heady elation at being able to make more and more decisions for myself. To be sure, I felt the awesome responsibility of having to make choices, some of which were crucial; but I also experienced a soaring sense of freedom. The earlier teachings of parents and church enabled me to discipline my elation fairly well. Sadly, uncurbed exuberance arising from newfound freedom can lead to unwise decisions and tragic results.

In Jesus' story, the young man had not gained the maturity and wisdom to make good decisions. He probably looked at his small fortune as easy come, easy go. He could live lavishly today; tomorrow would take care of itself. His experience of too much too soon played its way out to a predictable conclusion. His lack of foresight and moderation almost would prove to be fatal.

The irony of the young man's decisions and actions is that he left home to be free but found himself enslaved by a spendthrift and reckless lifestyle. He had exchanged true freedom in his father's house for slavery to himself and to his own whims. He had forged his own chains on the anvil of selfish indulgence. His life had turned out to be nothing like what he had envisioned as he had stepped out on the road and had taken the first swift, confident, thrilling steps away from home.

Remember that the younger son likely represented the tax collectors and sinners with whom Jesus ate and to whom He reached out. He did not excuse their wrongs. By their choices, they had moved away from God; they had broken His Commandments. Ethically and morally, they had rejected or ignored God's standards for living. Perhaps some of the people labeled "sinners" were morally good people who simply had despaired of keeping the burdensome regulations of the added oral tradition that had made the law a heavy load God never intended. Yet in the religious leaders' eyes, these people Jesus gladly welcomed into fellowship with Him were riffraff—worthless outcasts, the scum of Jewish society. In Jesus' eyes, they were people who needed God's forgiveness and were well worth His grace.

At what points in the first scene of Jesus' mural—the younger son's leaving home—do we see ourselves? In the first verses of Jesus' story, I think many of us catch more than a casual glimpse of ourselves in the younger son's attitudes and actions if we have the courage and honesty to look carefully.

First, we easily can become and remain the center of our worlds. "Give me" can become the theme of our prayers to the Father and of our approach to others. For a large part of my life, one of my struggles has been to overcome selfishness. Along the way, I have been helped to see my tendency to be self-centered. I really want to be more caring, sensitive, and generous. Getting there is not easy. The words *I, me, my,* and *mine* have a way of being too prominent in my vocabulary. I continue to work on abandoning the false notion that everything and everybody revolve around me. I really want to become more others-centered in meaningful service. What about you?

In a real sense, the younger son used his father to achieve the son's goal. Sadly, professing Christians can seek to use God to fulfill selfish purposes. Years ago, a neighbor confidently said she was praying that God would enable her and her husband to own a house with a swimming pool. Even today, a distorted theology presents God as the ready dispenser of new cars, finer houses, salary increases, and executive positions to faithful believers (and contributors to various "ministries"). To seek to use God to fulfill selfish aims is an extremely dangerous venture.

Tragically, self-centeredness also views others as objects to be manipulated rather than as persons of worth to be valued, loved, and served. When one is consumed with self, no real, meaningful relationships are possible, for other people are merely instruments to be collected, used, and discarded when they no longer are of benefit. Self-centeredness has room for only one person.

As likely the younger son did in relation to his father, we easily can see our relationship with God to be defined by restraints that limit life. The eight "don'ts" and the two "do's" in the Ten Commandments can blind us to the tremendous freedoms we have in the broader arena of our lives. We can lose sight of the truth that some areas of life are roped off for a reason: our own good. When we resist the temptations to cross God's lines, we are freed to cooperate with Him as He helps us become what He designed us to be: His children, serving Him by serving others and thus maturing spiritually. Rather than limiting life, God pushes back the boundaries, enlarging and enriching our experiences with Him. God is not busily at work making sure we do not have too much fun; He is at work creating and sustaining the deep joy and fulfillment of life lived in His love.

What may appear to be God's restraints really are designed to protect us from ourselves as we are driven by the conviction that we know what is best for us. Only God knows the results of sin without experiencing sin. We do not know until we commit sin, and then we must experience the disastrous consequences. Thus, God seeks to protect us from sin's devastation, not to prevent our happiness.

As the younger son learned, what we perceive to be freedom actually can be another form of slavery. We can come under the power of our pursuit of pleasure, prominence, or acceptance. The apostle Paul quoted people in the church at Corinth who evidently believed they could indulge in immoral physical gratification without affecting their essential selves. "'Everything is permissible for me'—but I will not be mastered by anything" (1 Cor. 6:12). The words in single quotes were the people's assertion; what follows was Paul's response. We can engage in self-indulgence, only to discover that self-indulgence rules us. Self-gratification is a cruel master that enslaves rather than liberates.

Also, as likely the younger son did, we can view freedom in negative rather than in positive terms. We can think in terms of freedom *from* what we perceive to be suffocating regimen and demand instead of freedom *to* become more than we are. After writing that we want to organize our lives as we see fit and to call this freedom, Emil Brunner stated: "I am not saying that freedom is not precious or necessary. My question is only: freedom from what? Freedom for what? Free from prejudice, free from compulsion, free from other people—marvelous! But free from God—this is the primary lie, the fountain of all evil."[8] The interesting paradox presented in the New Testament is that freedom is found in slavery—we become truly free when we become servants (bond slaves) of Christ. When we place our faith in Him, we are free to become all He can make of us as we cooperate with Him. He frees us from sin's penalty and power, and He frees us to realize a glorious destiny in Him.

We can see ourselves in the younger son's view of freedom as doing what he pleased. "And what is there more thrilling than to do as we like, to live it up! For many people, this is the highest goal. A secret longing for such unlimited freedom burns in all of us and leads us astray again and again. . . . My will be done, I am my own lord and master. Such obstinacy, such egotism, stirs in the heart of each of us, and it is the root of all sin."[9]

Who of us has not made the younger son's headstrong, stubborn insistence—by actions or words—that we will do things our way? A song popular many years ago and still sometimes heard celebrates a lifetime of doing as a person pleased. With more than a hint of pride, the singer declares that he has flaunted convention, rules, and standards and has done as he saw fit—even if others got hurt in the process. As he approaches the end of his life, he has few regrets about what he has done. He has tasted life to the full on his own terms. He persistently did things his way. Each of us faces the choice of doing life our way or God's way. We are free to choose our approach. We are not free to choose the results. Our choice works its way out to inevitable consequences.

The younger son would do as he pleased, whatever might come. When we take an I-will-do-what-I-want-no-matter-what attitude toward our actions and relationships, we place ourselves solidly in the center of our worlds. A right relationship with our Heavenly Father through Jesus Christ means that we replace our self-will,

---

[8] Emil Brunner, *Sowing and Reaping: The Parables of Jesus* (Richmond: John Knox Press, 1965), 36.
[9] Ibid., 36-37.

self-assertion, and self-absorption with loving trust in and obedience to Him

Again, to me an implication in Jesus' vivid word picture in verses 11-13 is that God does not want us to remain dependent, passive children. I think a sharp difference exists between healthy and unhealthy dependence on God. To be sure, in a real sense we depend on God for everything—life, health, energy, food, opportunity, and inner strength. Above all, we depend on Him for salvation and sustaining grace. I agree with the statement that "no person ever becomes so mature that he can declare his independence of God."[10] We need Him, daily and desperately. Yet I believe God wants us to grow and develop as His children—to mature into healthy spiritual adulthood under His guidance and care. I think He wants to help us maximize our abilities, stretch our intellects, deepen our faith, and strengthen our courage. When we encounter difficulties, face problems, or experience crises, I do not believe He wants us to stand idly by in an expectation that He will fix the situation. I do believe deeply that He wants us to apply the skills and the intellect He has given us, to weigh options, to use available resources, to consult trusted and able people, and to pray that He will give us wisdom, strength, and guidance. We legitimately can pray for Him to open doors, but we cannot expect Him to carry us through them! To ask His help while we work at solutions is valid; simply to expect Him to do all the work and to provide us with neatly packaged remedies while we merely wait inactively is not legitimate. In fact, much that presently is presented in the guise of faith is dependence on magic—wanting God to act as the Great Genie who magically gives us what we want. If God did everything for us, we would not grow; we would remain immature.

As did the younger son, we can distance ourselves from God and move into far countries of our choosing. God will honor our choices. In Romans 11:22, Paul wrote: "Consider . . . the kindness and sternness [severity] of God; sternness to those who fell, but kindness to you, provided that you continue in his kindness." God's great kindness is His giving us the freedom to choose; His sternness or severity is the other side of the same coin: We must choose, and we are responsible for our choices. Paul's Gentile

---

[10] Tolbert, 125.

readers had accepted God's offer of grace in Christ—His overwhelming kindness. As a whole, the Jews had rejected Jesus; and the result for them was self-chosen judgment. People who respond positively to God's grace see Him as kind; individuals who refuse that grace view God as severe or stern because they experience judgment. We can choose to distance ourselves from God. He never will stop caring for us, but He will honor our choice.

If we choose to distance ourselves from God, we move away from our true home. The first time I really was away from home was when I went to seminary in New Orleans, Louisiana. Even when I was in college, I was only 25 miles from home. I could go home almost any time I chose. That was not the case when I was in seminary. I was only about 100 miles away, but the distance might as well have been 1,000 miles. I had no car, and my work and classroom schedules tied me tightly to New Orleans. I still consider the first year there to be the loneliest period in my life—truly a dark night of my soul in which I faced almost overwhelming demands alone. For the first time, I knew how missing home felt, and I became much more appreciative of home and family, as the younger son would come to be.

To be in a close relationship with God is to be at home—with Him, others, and ourselves. To be away from Him is to be homeless in the deepest sense. The chorus of the hymn "Softly and Tenderly" captures well the idea of God's continuing invitation to people away from Him by choice: "Come home, come home, Ye who are weary come home; Earnestly, tenderly, Jesus is calling, Calling, O sinner, come home!"[11]

A final glimpse of our faces in the first scene of Jesus' mural is in the younger son's wasting his father's money. In that action, we are reminded that we can squander the wealth God has given us. Our lives are gifts from Him. Our time, energy, abilities, and opportunities come from Him. He gives spiritual gifts to people of faith. With His gifts comes the responsibility to manage them well. We can use them to honor Him and to help others, or we can waste them—throw them away by lavishing them on ourselves. The result is spiritual poverty.

---

[11] Will L. Thompson, "Softly and Tenderly" (No. 312, *The Baptist Hymnal*, 1991)

Eli Landrum

In the first scene of Jesus' story, we see something of ourselves. More importantly, we see a great deal about God. He is the ideal, perfect Father who provides all we have and affirms us as persons. Instead of overriding our freedom to choose, He honors it. He wants us to be in His family as His children, but only if that is what we freely choose.

Scene 2: A Reversal of Fortune (Vv. 14-16)

14 *"After he had spent everything, there was a severe famine in that whole country, and he began to be in need.* **15** *So he went and hired himself out to a citizen of that country, who sent him to his fields to feed pigs.* **16** *He longed to fill his stomach with the pods that the pigs were eating, but no one gave him anything."*

For an unspecified length of time, the younger son lived his fantasy. His extravagant and reckless spending, however, depleted his resources. We would be hard pressed to find anywhere else in literature a comparable account with such brevity and yet with such graphic imagery. With startlingly few but expertly applied brush strokes, Jesus painted the scene of the young man's plunge from the heights of delight to the depths of despair. The movement is swift and all downhill.

After a time of high living, the younger son spent his last coin. The Greek word translated "spent" (v. 14) also can be rendered "squandered." The root verb means "to tear," "to devour," "to consume by extravagance." It can mean "to spend," "to waste." The idea is that lavish and unwise spending had eaten up the young man's financial means. J. B. Phillips translated the words: "He had run trough all his money."[1] Note that Jesus gave no specifics concerning how the young man had spent his money; He simply stated that the younger son had been extravagant, free-spending.

When the young man's pockets were empty, "a severe famine" gripped the entire region in which he was living. The Greek word rendered "severe" has the idea of strength, power, or might. The famine was devastating. "He began to be in need"—literally, he began to fall behind in having what was necessary to survive; he lacked the basics of life; he ran short of resources. The *Holman Christian Standard Bible* translates: "He had nothing."[2] Clarence Jordan translated the words, "He was really hard up."[3] What a stunning reversal of fortune! At home, he had enjoyed access to plenty. He had shared his father's bounty, so he never had to worry about life's necessities. He had taken his next meal for granted. He had left home with his pockets full and his heart light. He had reveled in his newfound freedom and for all-too-brief a time had enjoyed the life about which he had dreamed. Then empty pockets issued in an empty stomach, and both were matched by the emptiness of his soul. The younger son found himself in dire circumstances "not only because he had lost his portion, but also

---

[1] Phillips, 159.
[2] *Holman Christian Standard Bible* (Nashville: Holman Bible Publishers, 2004), 886.
[3] Jordan, 62.

because he now had no inner support or stay, nothing spiritual to fall back on."[4]

Evidently the young man still was determined to rebound from his misfortunes on his own. He probably hung on desperately to the stubborn belief that he could ride out the lean times and realize his dream of continued freedom centered in financial independence. Perhaps he could rebuild his fortune. No doubt he had worked hard on his father's farm, and he could do so again until he recovered. Then he would resume living his dream of the good life.

How frantically the young man must have searched for employment that would enable him to survive! In itself that must have been a traumatic comedown for a person who had thrown money around with abandon. He merely was beginning to descend into the depths, however. In the Greek text, the phrase "hired himself out" (v. 15) literally is "was attached to." He attached himself to a resident of the area. The Greek term has the idea of being glued to or joined to the "citizen." Marvin R. Vincent wrote that the phrase implies "he *forced himself* upon the citizen, who was unwilling to engage him, and who took him into service only upon persistent entreaty."[5] The young man's desperation is reflected in his refusal to take "no" for an answer. He was destitute and hungry; starvation was a real possibility. Perhaps for the first time in his life, he stared death in the face. His will to survive landed him a job from a reluctant employer.

The employer sent the young man "to feed pigs." Again, Marvin R. Vincent suggested that because the young man had persisted so strongly in pressing for a job, the farmer finally had given in and hired him. Then the employer "gave him the meanest possible employment."[6] The young man found himself performing the most menial, humiliating, and repugnant task at hand.

The job represented to the young man what hitting absolute bottom means to addicts in our day. He was humiliated and reduced to life's lowest rung. Accepting the task was a denial of his

---

[4] R. C. H. Lenski, *The Interpretation of St. Luke's Gospel* (Columbus, Ohio: The Wartburg Press, 1946), 810.
[5] Marvin R. Vincent, "The Gospel According to Luke" in *Word Studies in the New Testament,* vol. 1 (Grand Rapids, Michigan: Wm. B. Eerdmans Publishing Co., 1965), 386.
[6] Ibid., 386.

religion. Leviticus 11:7-8 states: "The pig, though it has a split hoof completely divided, does not chew the cud; it is unclean for you. You must not eat their meat or touch their carcasses; they are unclean for you." (See also Deut. 14:8.) The Jewish Talmud contains the statement: "Cursed be the man who breeds swine."[7] Joachim Jeremias pointed out that the prodigal "could not have observed the Sabbath: hence he must have been reduced to the lowest depths of degradation and practically forced to renounce the regular practice of his religion."[8] No Jew could sink lower than to tend pigs. In today's terminology, the young man wound up in the gutter, the skid row of his day. The Jewish religious leaders who listened to Jesus' story would have shuddered in revulsion; to them, the young man would have been beyond redemption.

Pathetically, the son who had left his father and his home to be free now served a second master. He first had become a slave to himself and his unthinking, selfish lifestyle; now he was dependent on a stranger for survival. He had traded plenty for poverty, freedom for demeaning drudgery, and a place of honor for shame and disgrace.

In verse 16 Jesus painted the young man's predicament in poignant hues. The younger son was so desperately hungry that he wanted to eat the pigs' feed. The "pods" were the fruit of the carob tree. The word *carob* literally means "little horn"; the carob pods were shaped like small horns. The pods could grow to be a foot long. Inside them was a sweet-tasting, gelatinous substance. The pods were used as feed for animals, and poor people sometimes ate the pods to survive. Carob pods became known as St. John's bread because of the tradition that John the Baptist ate such pods in the wilderness. John Nolland, however, has suggested that the "pods" in verse 16 may not have been those known as St. John's bread. They may have been "its wild cousin, which was much smaller and whose fruit was bitter and was not eaten except in desperation."[9] In either view, the younger son was ravenously hungry and fast approaching death. He would eat anything that would enable him to survive.

---

[7] Joachim Jeremias, *The Parables of Jesus* (London: SCM Press Ltd, 1963), 129.
[8] Ibid.
[9] John Nolland, "Luke 9:21–18:34," vol. 35b in *Word Biblical Commentary* (Dallas, Texas: Word Books, Publisher, 1993),783.

The closing words of verse 16 are haunting: "No one gave him anything." Clarence Jordan rendered the statement in contemporary terms: "Nobody was giving him even a hand-out."[10] The tense of the Greek verb translated "gave" conveys continuous action: people repeatedly refused to give the young man food. Robert H. Stein suggested that the words "he longed . . . but no one gave him anything" are open to several interpretations: "This may mean that he saw the pigs eating and being filled and he would have liked to have been full also. It was psychologically impossible, however, for him to eat such 'pigfood.' It could also mean that he would have liked to have eaten the food the pigs ate, but it was physiologically impossible to do so since humans could not eat such food. Finally, it could mean that he would have liked to have eaten the food the pigs ate, but the 'citizen' would not allow him to do so."[11] He wanted to eat the carob pods, but he either could not do so or could not bring himself to do so.

The words "no one gave him anything" are an eerie echo of David's words written centuries earlier: "Look to my right and see; no one is concerned for me. I have no refuge; no one cares for my life" (Ps. 142:4). The young man had been somebody at home and during the time he had money to throw around in the land to which he had fled. Now that he was broke, he was reduced to a nobody. Fair-weather friends who had been more than happy to benefit from his money distanced themselves from him. He was a Jew among Gentiles, an alien who did not merit their sympathy or help. Thus, the citizens of the area consistently refused to help the desperate young man. They would not even give him scraps of food to sustain him.

No doubt, the prodigal had numbers of so-called friends when he was tossing money around with reckless abandon. I well can imagine the rather large entourage and the many hangers-on who accompanied him as he provided entertainment and pleasure with his steadily dwindling supply of money. When he was destitute, where were they? Perhaps at this point he began to consider the truth that his father never would have abandoned him; the father he had left had always stood by him. Maybe the son began to

---

[10] Jordan, 62.
[11] Robert H. Stein, "Luke" in *The New American Commentary*, vol. 24 (Nashville: Broadman Press, 1992), 405.

realize what he had given up in his pursuit of his conception of the good life.

I have wondered whether Jesus' poignant emphasis that no one helped the younger son was directed toward the Pharisees and scribes at this early point in His story. In Matthew 23, Jesus leveled withering words at them in an attempt to penetrate their religious armor and to jolt them into awareness of where they were spiritually and of their need of grace. In the process, Jesus said: "They [the religious leaders] tie up heavy loads that are hard to carry and put them on people's shoulders, but they themselves aren't willing to lift a finger to move them" (Matt. 23:4, HCSB). The religious leaders shunned people they viewed as irreligious. The Pharisees and scribes could have reached out to the tax collectors and sinners in an effort to reclaim them. Not only were the religious leaders not doing so, but they also were incensed that Jesus—who clearly indicated He represented God—would offer God's acceptance to them. To the religious leaders, this was heresy of the first order that they could not tolerate. They could not let Jesus' attitude and actions go unchallenged. Conversely, He could not let their lack of concern for others go unchallenged.

In Jesus' story, the younger son's descent into ruin was stunningly swift. His downward mobility accelerated pathetically. Self-will had led to separation from his father and from home. Reckless abandon had issued in poverty. Poverty was deepened by famine, and the result for the prodigal was gnawing hunger. Desperation had driven him to tend pigs, the only job he could find; and taking the job meant that he degraded himself. The people of his adopted land turned him away. He had come to the end of his rope; he had reached bottom. Emil Brunner characterized the younger son's descent in this manner: "First, there is inner disintegration, then outer misery, and finally total ruin, the abyss."[12]

We can see ourselves in the second scene of Jesus' mural—if we will. As did the young man's, our choices always have consequences, and we are responsible for our choices. The younger son had no one to blame for his situation but himself. Our days involve making one choice after another in rapid succession. Some choices are made quickly, almost without thought, and concern

---

[12] Brunner, 37.

daily routines and inconsequential matters. Other choices are more significant; we must weigh them seriously, for they affect others as well as ourselves. Moral, ethical, and spiritual choices shape who we are and determine the depth of our characters and the degree of positive and negative impact we have on others. When we ultimately answer to God, we will be responsible for our choices that issued in our characters and destinies.

The words "he . . . spent everything" (v. 14)—squandered his resources—present us with a haunting question about how we are managing the currency of our lives in our marketplaces—currency that comes from God. Everything we have comes as gifts from Him. We often state that truth and express gratitude to Him. Yet words of gratitude without consistent and sound stewardship are hollow. He gives us abilities or talents, intellect, physical strength, opportunities, and material goods. We can waste these resources frivolously or we can use them to enrich our lives and the lives of family members and people with legitimate needs. We can invest these resources in Christ's redemptive purpose. The question is whether we will squander the currency of our lives or invest it in something that is eternal.

The second scene in Jesus' mural depicts vividly separation from God and its results. When we choose our own way in a quest for freedom from the Father, we alienate ourselves from Him. The lesson is that moving away from God always leads to disaster. Always. In Jesus' story, the son's first step away from his father was movement toward crisis. The writer of Proverbs was right: "There is a way that seems right to a man, but in the end it leads to death" (Prov. 16:25). Leslie D. Weatherhead, a noted English Methodist pastor of a former generation, wrote: "All roads lead to disaster which lead away from Him [Christ]."[13] The statement holds true of walking away from God. Moving away from God results in emptiness far worse than physical hunger. Separation from Him produces a spiritual hunger—a famine of the soul—that only His love and mercy can satisfy. Conversely, when we choose the path toward Him, we find that it leads to relationship with Him. That relationship issues in full life now and hereafter.

---

[13] Leslie D. Weatherhead, *Over His Own Signature* (London: Epworth Press, 1960), 48.

The Compassionate Father

For a person to deliberately turn his or her back on the Father's love and to reject His care and provision to be his own man or her own woman diminishes that individual progressively. Life turned in on itself grows smaller; it withers as self absorption saps its vitality. To spurn God's love is to reduce life to a level God never intended. Lives slogging through today's equivalents of pigs' sties are antitheses of God's intention for persons made in His image. He wants people to have full life in relationship with Him. Real life begins with an openness to accept God's love for us.

When we look closely at Jesus' word picture, we see the tragic truth that we can turn away from a love that gives us everything we need; we can exchange generous provision for reliance on our own abilities and on the uncertain and arbitrary whims of other people's benevolence, which misguided reliance often leaves us empty and destitute. The father in Jesus' story provided for his son's needs during the entire time the son was at home. Then the father gave the young man the son's part of the inheritance. The contrast between the father's generosity and the closed-fist response of the people in the far country is striking. I think Jesus deliberately presented a stark picture of a bad trade—swapping a father's loving provision for inevitable destitution and hunger. The father gave freely to his son; in the son's desperate struggle to survive, "no one gave him anything" (Luke 15:16). Everyone turned him away.

For most people in the distant country, the poverty-stricken young man evidently was an unwelcome, unwanted problem undeserving of their assistance. He literally had nothing, and people repeatedly refused his requests for food. Most of them may have had limited resources, and they were unwilling to share the little they had. Yet implied in Jesus' words was an unwillingness on the part of some who could have helped.

Later, in Luke 16:19-31, Jesus told the story of the rich man and Lazarus. A beggar named Lazarus sat at a rich man's gate, wanting only the leftovers from the wealthy man's table in order to survive. Every day, on leaving and entering his house, the rich man passed Lazarus but never really saw him. Evidently, he accepted Lazarus as merely a blight on the landscape of his world—a blight that if ignored might go away. Jesus' story gives no indication the rich man extended any help to Lazarus. To use the tragic truth that the poor are always with us (see John 12:8) as an excuse to do nothing to alleviate poverty is to deny the spirit of the One who identifies with "the least" of His "brothers" (Matt. 25:40).

Jesus' story of the rich man and Lazarus contains a striking parallel to our time and calls for decision. That story and Jesus' description of the younger son's plight in the distant country present to us in sharp detail the awfulness of physical poverty. One of the glaring problems of our day is the rapidly widening gap between the haves and the have-nots, between the comfortable and well-off and the desperately poor. As was true in Jesus' day—and as in the case of the prodigal—many people literally live on the edge of existence. Compounding the problem is the almost nonchalant attitude—and even resentment—of "the haves" toward the poor. Christians must continue to address the problem of poverty and to seek to meet the needs of the poor among us.

Yet as devastating as physical poverty is, a worse poverty exists, and it is spiritual in nature. Among the glaring ills of our culture is a destitution of soul. Indications of inner emptiness—such as the frantic quest for youth, acquisition, power, and pleasure—abound. Among the increasing evidences are the accelerating obsession with entertainment and the accompanying cult of "celebrityism"—both secular and religious. Trying to fill inner emptiness by vicarious stardom points to spiritual poverty—a dislike for who one is and an attempt to replace that with something or someone else. Yet even the spotlight's reflected glow inevitably will dim, and the emptiness will remain. It can only be filled with the Father's love and acceptance. We can consign ourselves to a poverty far worse than lack of material necessities, but we do so against the Father's wishes.

Scene 3: A Moment of Truth (Vv. 17-20a)

17 *"When he came to his senses, he said, 'How many of my father's hired men have food to spare, and here I am starving to death!* **18** *I will set out and go back to my father and say to him: Father, I have sinned against heaven and against you.* **19** *I am no longer worthy to be called your son; make me like one of your hired men.'* **20a** *So he got up and went to his father."*

Scene 2 of Jesus' riveting mural ended with the gaunt, ragged, and desperate younger son hungrily eying the carob pods on which pigs were feeding. The colors Jesus used are dark, somber, and depressing. The sky is overcast, and no light filters through. The haggard figure tending pigs is pitiable and broken. Scene 3 begins with the first rays of sunlight breaking through the dark clouds. Jesus introduced the abrupt turnaround with the word "when" (v. 17). The Greek text literally has "but." The *New International Version's* translation of the Greek adversative *de* as "when" does not convey the sharp turning point—the stark contrast—Jesus introduced. No doubt the young man felt deep humiliation and self-loathing. He was in a desperate situation from which he could not extricate himself—*but* suddenly a glimmer of hope burst into the darkness of his plight. He had been mired in despair and hopelessness, teetering on the ragged edge of existence, but he reached a critical turning point.

The phrase "came to his senses"—literally "having come to himself"—conveys a great deal more than the young man's finally beginning to think straight, though that was a necessary step in a deeper process. Malcolm O. Tolbert clearly stated the beginning of the process. He wrote that at this point the third parable of Jesus in Luke 15 differs from the other two stories. In the first two parables, the focus is on people's search for something they had lost. In the third parable, a person is lost, and "he cannot be found until he . . . desires to be found. It was necessary for him to **come to himself**—to emerge from the dream world of unreality and illusion into which had fled in order to see himself and his situation in a true light. Now he understands what he had given up when he had in effect renounced his sonship. . . . He also sees how wicked was the pride and how selfish the motivations that led him to turn his back on his father."[1] Such sound thinking contributed to the deeper experience of repentance. Robert H. Stein wrote: "This [coming to himself] is a Hebrew/Aramaic expression for 'repented.' This refers not only to a mental process that causes him to think more clearly about his situation but also to a moral renewal involving repentance."[2] Even interpreters who view the phrase "came to his senses" as simply a moment of clarity in which he

---

[1] Tolbert, 125-6.
[2] Stein, 406.

became fully aware of what he had done and of the only option open to him acknowledge that the experience involved shades or overtones of repentance.

One speculation is that self-loathing played a role in the young man's reaching the point of repentance. Yet "he could not have hated himself unless there had been a good man in him to do the hating."[3] We well can imagine that when the full impact of what the young man had done hit him, he felt a torrent of emotions: shame, self-judgment, guilt, and remorse. No doubt he became aware of how far he had strayed from being the son he should have been and probably, deep down, really wanted to be. Not only was he hungry, but he also was in pain because of his thoughtless decisions and actions. Yet "the repentance of the lost son is . . . not something merely negative. In the last analysis, it is not merely disgust; it is above all homesickness; not just turning away from something, but turning back home."[4]

The young man knew that back home, his father's "hired men" had more than enough to eat—literally, they were "surrounded by loaves"[5] (v. 17). In contrast, the younger son was "starving to death." He decided he would get up and return to his father and to his true home (v. 18). Did he also long for his mother's soothing, loving touch? Joiachim Jeremias stated that "an oriental would not think it suitable to mention the mother, but she is included here, as a matter of course, and also in what follows."[6] The thought of abundant food in his father's house led the prodigal to decide to go back home, but it likely was the strong pull of home itself that exerted the greatest force. Gnawing hunger was mixed with intense longing.

Some readers and interpreters have questioned the father's lack of action in seeking his son. As time passed and the son still had not returned, would not a caring father have begun a search for his son? Such questioners maintain that here the parallels between

---

[3] George Arthur Buttrick, "The Gospel According to St. Luke" in *The Interpreter's Bible*, vol. 8 (Nashville: Abingdon Press, 1952), 272-3.
[4] Thielicke, 26.
[5] Archibald Thomas Robertson, "The Gospel According to Luke" in *Word Pictures in the New Testament*, vol. II (Nashville: Broadman Press, 1930), 210.
[6] Joachim Jeremias, *Rediscovering the Parables* (London: SCM Press LTD, 1966), 102.

The Compassionate Father

God and the human father no longer hold. Further questions must be asked, however: What if the father had gone after his son in the far country and had found him before the son hit bottom? Could the father have forced his son to return home? Even if he could have done so, what would the son's disposition have been? In the first two parables in Luke 15, active seeking was involved: the shepherd searched for the lost sheep, and the woman looked frantically for her lost coin. The third parable injects the element of human choice. One of Jesus' points in the parable was that the son had to decide on his own to go back home. Only then would he really be at home in his father's house. Actually, only then could the son be at home with himself. Jesus was pointing out to the tax collectors and sinners as well as to the religious leaders that their entering a relationship with God could become a reality only if they turned to Him in an act of their wills. Consciously and deliberately, they had to repent—to turn from their sins and turn to God and home.

Again, some interpreters have questioned the son's motive in deciding to return to his father. The young man was at the end of his rope; he had to have something to eat. His consuming thought was to survive. He had nowhere to turn and no one to whom he could go—except his father. Thus, some commentators have suggested that the young man's motive in his decision to return home was basically selfish—to survive and to improve his lot in life. Better to put up with his father's directives and to eat well than to starve to death! Better a drab, bland life on the farm than no life at all!

Before we are too harsh on the prodigal, we need to reflect on the truths that seldom if ever are our motives unmixed and that desperation can—and has—caused people to turn to God. In recounting their conversion experiences, countless people have told about reaching points of utter hopelessness and helplessness. They literally had nowhere to turn and no one to whom they could go. They had come to the end of their resources, the end of their ropes; they saw no light in the intense darkness of their lives; they and no one else could put the pieces of their shattered lives back together; or they had made such a terrible mess of their lives they felt self-hatred and were certain no one could or would love them, least of all God. Some seriously contemplated suicide as the only way out of their misery. Yet they reached out for God and found

Him receptive and forgiving. They discovered that even when He is the last resort, God will answer people's cries for help with love and grace. Sometimes, only crushing crises will move people to turn to God. Leslie D. Weatherhead stated this profound truth well: "So often it is true to say that the grace of God makes no difference to man until he is desperate and broken."[7] George A. Buttrick wrote: "The hunger motive . . . was savingly entangled with memories of a father's love, and with shame for the turpitude which had flouted love."[8]

Some people are driven to God by a deep hunger for something more than they have found in their worldly pursuits. Nothing they have done or have accumulated has given lasting satisfaction. I consider one of my favorite cartoons to be a contemporary parable about a prevalent approach to life in our time. The setting is Christmas morning. A little boy sits atop a mound of toys and asks, "Is this all?" Today, a prevailing question many adults are asking is, "How many toys equal happiness and fulfillment?" The failure of success, money, fame, acquisition, power, and shallow relationships to bring fulfillment have caused some in our society to begin questioning whether at life's end, the person with the most toys really wins. "Wins what?" they ask. Their disillusionment with material things causes them to consider a deeper dimension to life: the spiritual aspect. In their desperate quest for identity, inner peace, wholeness, relief from guilt, and a sense of satisfaction, they have turned to any number of religions, philosophies, and self-help books and programs. Many have turned to the Scriptures and to the Christ of the Scriptures and have found that He fills the yawning void in their lives.

I applaud people who give testimonies of turning to God out of desperation and a sense of something vital missing from their lives. Overwhelming need brought them to their moments of truth. Their dramatic experiences of finding God when they reached bottom and of receiving His grace have telling impact on others who need to know that no matter what they have done, they can get up and go to God. Thankfully, however, their emotion-charged conversion stories do not define the parameters of the salvation

---

[7] Leslie D. Weatherhead, *In Quest of a Kingdom* (Nashville: Abingdon Press, 1944), 23.
[8] Buttrick, *The Parables of Jesus*, 93.

experience. My story is different and less exciting. In a way, I was like the Jews' religious leaders Jesus addressed: in a sense, not far from the kingdom of God, with the advantage of exposure to God's revelation and ample opportunities to respond positively. I was not far, but neither was I in. I needed to arrive at the point of definite decision.

I must write about my salvation experience in terms of what has been called religion's preventive impact. I practically was raised in the local Southern Baptist church in my small Mississippi town (and in some part, in the local Methodist church as young people from both churches attended each church's youth events). I was helped toward what I have come to consider a gentle or nurtured conversion while I was yet a preteen. Caring people taught and modeled standards and values that remain significant parts of my life. These people helped me avoid many destructive actions, habits, and attitudes and with patience and kindness guided me toward faith in Christ. Do not get me wrong. I had done my share of sinning. I had taken things that were not mine; I had shaded the truth on occasions when to do so was to my advantage; I had disobeyed my parents; I had been unkind and even cruel to some of my peers. Yet at such a young age I had no consciousness of what were considered deep and glaring sins.

I was helped to see that no matter how good I perceived myself to be, I nevertheless was a sinner who needed God's saving grace in Christ. I needed to make a deliberate decision to repent and to place my faith in Christ. I reached my moment of truth. In my own way; I came to myself. I accepted Jesus as my Savior and committed my life to Him. I arrived at my moment of truth by a different route from the young man in Jesus' story, but the decision was the same: to go to the Father and home. No matter how we come to our moments of truth—to ourselves and to repentance— we must do so if we are to enter a redemptive relationship with God. We must turn to God and home.

The young man in Jesus' riveting story said, "I will set out and go back to my father"—literally, "having arisen I will go to my father" (v. 18). He immediately would get up from the mire of the pig sty—he would climb out of the gutter—and start home. The words "I will" convey determined decision. Then the young man framed what he would say to his father. I agree with interpreters who state that what follows demonstrates the sincerity of the young man's repentance. The words convey much more than insincere, shallow pretense designed to obtain the father's desired resources. The son wanted more than a meal; he wanted a restored relationship with his father.

No doubt the son's first words to his father would be the hardest to say: "I have sinned." Awareness of the magnitude of having turned his back on his father led first to confession. Confession preceded request. The Greek term translated "sinned" is the common word for sin in the New Testament. The root verb means "to miss the mark." It was a shooter's word for missing or falling short of a target. It came to mean "to be in error," "to be mistaken." Then it took on the idea of missing or wandering off the path of righteousness and honor, of doing or going wrong. The young man's honest admission to himself was that in turning his back on his father, he had gone terribly wrong, and he would confess this truth to his father.

The penitent son's choice of words is significant. He confessed that he had sinned against "heaven" and against his father. The term "heaven" was an oblique reference to God. God's name became so sacred to the Jews that they avoided saying or writing it; they substituted words and phrases to refer to God. In Jesus' story, the young man acknowledged that his first and greatest sin had been against God. He had not been what God intended him to be—a faithful, obedient son to his father; a man who kept God's Commandments; and an individual of maturing character.

The young man also had sinned against his father. He had caused his father indescribable anguish by rejecting the father, home, family, and family values. The son had brought shame on the family name. Worst of all, he had turned away from his father's love—the most painful rejection the father could experience.

The depth of the young man's repentance and the clarity with which he saw what he had done are reflected in the words he would say to his father: "I am no longer worthy to be called your son" (v. 19). Formerly he had not valued his relationship as a son in his father's house; now he recognized he had no claim to that relationship. "Earlier he was unwilling to be called a son; now he felt unworthy to be so called."[9] I do not think this admission was

---

[9] Frank Stagg, *Studies in Luke's Gospel* (Nashville: Convention Press, 1967), 103.

designed to touch the father and thereby gain the desired food and other necessities of life. Robert H. Stein paraphrased the son's planned statement this way: "A father like you deserves better than a son like me."[10] To me, the words that follow in the son's planned speech show his sincerity and humility.

I have wondered whether at this point in His story, Jesus was not trying to bring the Pharisees and the scribes to see that no person deserves to be included in God's family. Clearly, people guilty of moral and ethical wrong did not deserve inclusion; but neither did people who thought their religious correctness earned them places of honor. In particular, the Pharisees considered themselves to be deserving of God's acceptance and blessings because they kept the Ten Commandments and all the minute regulations in the oral tradition that had grown up around the Commandments. They felt they merited their right standing with God; therefore, God owed them something. In fact, the Pharisee in Jesus' parable in Luke 18:9-14 was not the only one who considered God fortunate to have him as an adherent.

Years ago, one of my favorite seminary professors was lecturing his class in New Testament studies. He described many Pharisees' attitude in a way I have never forgotten. He had us imagine two Pharisees meeting on the street. "How are you doing?" one man asked. "I'm way ahead," the second Pharisee responded. Because of his works of righteousness, he felt he had accumulated a stack of IOU's with God's signature on them. Many of the Pharisees of Jesus' day had reached the dangerous point of thinking they could put God in their debt by their religious works. Believers today are not immune to this misguided thinking. Because of their years of Bible study, worship, and service, they can feel that God owes them favors, especially when they find themselves in life's tight places. Ledger-entry religion remains a persistent misconception.

Jesus well may have been indicating that no one is worthy of God's love and mercy; we receive right standing with Him through sheer grace. Not only tax collectors and sinners needed to see that truth; the religious leaders also needed to take it to heart.

The young man in Jesus' story would implore his father, "Make me like one of your hired hands." In that day, three levels or tiers of slaves or servants existed. Slaves *(douloi,* bondslaves) were owned

---

[10] Stein, 406.

by their masters but generally were considered members of the family. Bondslaves supervised male and female servants *(paides* and *paidisdas).* The hired servants *(misthoi)* were the lowest tier of slaves. They were day laborers—hired hands who could be dismissed at any time and who were not considered to be members of the family. Their employment hinged on "the full range of natural forces, the seasonal needs of the production of crops, and the whims of the estate managers."[11] The son in Jesus' story would ask for a position whose continuation would depend on the quality of his work each day and on the father's fairness. He would not ask for a handout or make it easy on himself. "He does not envision a divine inheritance. He only wants to repair the separation, to live again in his father's house."[12] Alfred Plummer stated: "The repentance is as real and decided as the fall. He prepares full confession, but no excuse."[13] The younger son accepted full responsibility for what he had done.

We can easily overlook the significance of the absence of excuses from the son's planned confession and plea. No doubt he could have come up with some: He was young; the father should have put his foot down; the older brother was impossible to live with; the peer group in the distant country exercised undue influence and led him astray. Rather than seek to soften or minimize what he had done, the son would acknowledge his willful wrong: "I have sinned." Confession and repentance call for honesty, else they are meaningless.

The young man quickly acted on his decision: "He got up and went to his father" (v. 20). The journey back home would be long and difficult—physically and emotionally—but the son's first step was a turning point for him. He could have remained paralyzed in indecision, but he acted on his resolve and turned toward home. "Repentance is just such a turning. It is a turning from self-will and

---

[11] Joel B. Green, "The Gospel of Luke" in *The New International Commentary on the New Testament* (Grand Rapids, Michigan: William B. Eerdmans Publishing Company, 1997), 581.
[12] Brunner, 38.
[13] Alfred Plummer, "A Critical and Exegetical Commentary on the Gospel According to S. Luke" in *The International Critical Commentary* (Edinburgh: T. & T. Clark, 1964), 375.

self-indulgence; it is a turning toward God and a glad submission to his rule of love."[14]

In His economical use of words, Jesus did not describe the young man's long walk home. When he had left home, no doubt he had done so with a spring in his step, perhaps whistling or humming a tune. Now he doggedly put one weary foot ahead of the other in a determined if unsteady gait. In imagination, we can see him—gaunt, ragged, unkempt, and hollow-eyed—staggering along the road. He sleeps on hard ground at night. He begs for scraps of food and barely manages to get enough to keep him going. Over and over, he repeats the speech he will make to his father. Not all the perspiration that streams down his face comes from exertion. His mind tries to picture the scene when he finally comes face-to-face with his father. Will his father speak to him or acknowledge him in any way? Will he wave his son away, dismissing him to his own devices? Will the father say in the vernacular of that day what I often heard in a colloquialism of south Mississippi: "You made your bed; now you will have to lie in it"? Will the father feed him, allow him to rest, and then send him away? Will the father allow him to stay but keep a chilly distance between them? What kind of reception will the son receive, and will he have a chance to make his proposal? Each negative possibility heightens the young man's anxiety and apprehension. With troubling thoughts and swirling emotions, desperately wishing—and perhaps praying—for a good outcome, the son doggedly moves toward home.

Look closely at the third scene in Jesus' mural. The young son looks a lot like us. Separated from God, we were (or are) separated from our true selves. When we come to ourselves and repent (turn from sin and turn to God), we take the first step toward becoming the selves God designed us to be. He did not design us to slog through the muck and mire of life's pig sties. He designed us for relationship with Him, not peonage to cruel masters of our making or choosing. He intends that every person be His child, nurtured by His care. Coming to ourselves and coming to God are synonymous. A longing for God exists somewhere deep within us, and until we turn to Him, we deny our true selves and fail to realize our potential. We forfeit the matchless privilege of redemptive relationship with the Heavenly Father who wants the best for us.

---

[14] Tolbert, 126.

In our time, many people speak about finding themselves. In some cases, this may be a thinly disguised excuse for doing nothing meaningful or "loafing for a living." Yet such a statement may indicate the individuals are on a serious quest to discover their identities, a sense of purpose, or their vocational or social niches. Until they find themselves, they drift on a turbulent sea without anchor or haven. The good news is that every person can find his or her true self in God. Unless people turn to God, they will never become the selves He intends them to be and that deep down inside they want to be. In coming to God, individuals find themselves as people of worth whom God loves and in whom He sees boundless potential He can help them realize.

The scene Jesus painted emphasizes that the restlessness and emptiness many people feel are a longing for the Father and home. They have not found home in acquisitions, achievements, acclaim, power, and prestige. They are looking for the home that is found only in a relationship with the One who loves them supremely.

In the scene, we see clearly that turning to God and home is a conscious decision of the will. Whether we are guilty of gross sins or are morally good people who have not committed our lives to Christ, we must choose to invite Him into our lives as Savior and Lord. Doing so is a matter of the will.

As was the case with the prodigal, coming to ourselves or coming to our "senses" (v. 17) turns our thoughts to our true home and the Father's gracious and bountiful provisions. He gives us the supreme gift of His presence, of deep and continuing fellowship with Him, of inclusion in His family. He showers on His family members grace, mercy, and love. No person needs to hunger for acceptance, care, comfort, encouragement, and meaningful responsibilities. The Father's provision satisfies completely.

As was true with the prodigal, probably one of the most difficult admissions we must make in turning toward the Father and home is, "I have sinned." How many of us have great difficulty saying to God and others, "I was wrong"? Yet the confession up front that we have sinned is absolutely necessary in true repentance. Recognizing our guilt and admitting our sin lead to heartfelt repentance and restoration.

We must accept full responsibility for our condition of being separated from God, of turning our backs on Him and going our own ways. Trying to shift blame to someone or something else leaves us mired in our wrong. Adam and Eve were the first but by no means the last to attempt to pass the buck for sin. In Genesis 3, when God confronted them with their disobedience to His command, they tried to shift the blame elsewhere. Adam blamed Eve, calling her "the woman you [God] put here with me" (Gen. 3:12). By implication, Adam also blamed God. In essence Adam said that had God not created Eve, he would not have sinned. Eve countered that the serpent made her do it. No doubt the serpent looked around desperately for someone else to blame. In our day, blame for sin is shifted to the family, the neighborhood, peers, or society—anywhere but personal, willful choice. Even Satan and demons can be used in an attempt to avoid personal responsibility. Years ago, a popular comedian parodied a favorite excuse of people caught in wrongdoing: "The devil *made* me do it" (italics mine). James was clear about the source of sin: "Each one is tempted when, by his own evil desire, he is dragged away and enticed. Then, after desire has conceived, it gives birth to sin; and sin, when it is full-grown, gives birth to death" (Jas. 1:14-15). With David, every person must admit, "I have sinned against the Lord" (2 Sam. 12:13).

The scene in Jesus' mural confronts us with the truth that our sin first is sin against God. David became painfully aware of this truth following his committing adultery with Bathsheba. When Bathsheba became pregnant, David failed in his attempts to make it appear that Uriah, Bathsheba's husband and a soldier in David's army, was the father of the unborn child. David arranged to have Uriah killed in battle; then David took Bathsheba as his wife. The prophet Nathan confronted David with his sin, and sometime later David wrote Psalm 51, in which he stated to God: "Against you, you only, have I sinned" (v. 4). David knew he had sinned against Bathsheba, Uriah, and the people of Israel. Yet David also knew that all sin is first and foremost sin against God. When we sin against others, we sin against the God who created them in His image.

In the prodigal's planned confession and appeal is the plain truth that none of us is worthy to be God's child. None of us deserves His grace that includes us in His family. We cannot earn or force our way into any family, and we certainly cannot pile up enough points to gain entrance into God's family. The humility this truth generates paves the way for our turning to God and casting ourselves on His grace.

After the prodigal decided what he would do, he acted on his intention: "He got up and went to his father" (v. 20a). Good intentions are noble; they arise out of hearts that really want to do and say the right things and perform acts of service that benefit others. Yet for intentions to reach full flower, we must act decisively; we have to follow through. In my experience, if I do not move quickly to turn good intentions into positive actions, most often I fail to complete the process. My good intentions fade and die. When noble intentions arise, we need to get up and go, as the prodigal did.

Scene 4: A Homecoming (VV. 20b-24)

20b *"But while he was still a long way off, his father saw him and was filled with compassion for him; he ran to his son, threw his arms around him and kissed him.* **21** *The son said to him, 'Father, I have sinned against heaven and against you. I am no longer worthy to be called your son.'* **22** *But the father said to his servants, 'Quick! Bring the best robe and put it on him. Put a ring on his finger and sandals on his feet.* **23** *Bring the fattened calf and kill it. Let's have a feast and celebrate.* **24** *For this son of mine was dead and is alive again; he was lost and is found.' So they began to celebrate."*

The Compassionate Father

We do not know how many miles the younger son walked or how many hours he was on the road, only that he traveled a great distance (see v. 13). Finally, he came within sight of home. The prodigal's homecoming is one of the most poignantly beautiful and dramatic scenes in the Bible—actually, in all literature. In addition, few scenes reveal more of God than this one. No parable, Bible passage, or Bible book reveals God fully. I am convinced that not even the Bible as a whole reveals all God's nature. He retains for Himself a great deal of mystery. Our small minds cannot grasp the greatness, majesty, power, and holiness that characterize God. Yet He has made Himself known more than adequately in the Scriptures and in Jesus.

The observation has been made repeatedly that if somehow all Bibles were destroyed and only John 3:16 survived, we would have adequate revelation about God and His good news for us. In the same vein, I feel that if we only had Jesus' parable in Luke 15:11-32, we would have all we really need to know about God's character, how He views us, and our value to Him.

In Jesus' parable, the father's reception of his son gives us a clear glimpse into the great heart of God. For that we can be eternally grateful, because we need to be sure about His intentions toward us and how He sees us. Jesus' beautiful word picture leaves no doubt.

As the returning son came within sight of home, he must have felt a surge of mixed emotions. He had been thrilled and elated as he walked away; now he must have viewed home through new eyes of appreciation tinged with apprehension. The old homestead never looked so good to him, for there lived the parents who had loved and nurtured him. Perhaps they still had some love for him—or at least pity. Even the thought of a stodgy older brother could not lessen the thrill at the sight of home. Even if tears misted his eyes, home was a sight to behold.

How many times a day had the prodigal's father looked anxiously and longingly down the road along which his son had walked away, confident and eager and elated? I agree with interpreters who believe the implication of the words "while he was still a long way off, his father saw him" (v. 20b) is that the father constantly looked for his son to come down the road. Some time before, had the father stood looking down that road at the retreating figure of his son, hoping against hope that the boy would stop, turn around, and come back? Frequently, no doubt, the father found himself looking in the direction his son had gone. Then one day, the father saw a faraway shape on the road. As the figure grew larger and more distinct, the father's eyes widened and his heart quickened its beat. In spite of the son's dreadful appearance, the father recognized his son. "The delicate cue of familiar mannerisms known intuitively only to love revealed [the prodigal's] identity."[1]

In addition to the father's longing for his son, Jesus' words imply to me something of the father's pain during his son's absence. How many times during each day did the father's thoughts go to his absent son? How many sleepless nights were spent in anxious concern for the son's welfare? To me, the father's gaze down the road, hoping to catch sight of his son, expresses the truth that God agonizes over people who are separated from Him by sin and longs for their movement toward Him.

Years ago, in a seminary course, an insightful professor of New Testament introduced me to the truth that God suffers. Our words *care, concern, anguish, pain,* and *suffering* are inadequate to convey the depth of how God views and responds to people who are outside His circle of grace by stubborn choice. The words *grief* and *sorrow* communicate deep, sharp, searing inner pain; yet these terms cannot convey what God experiences in His love for people who deliberately have rejected Him. God is not unmoved by the plight of sinners. Robert L. Cargill insightfully wrote that the returning prodigal was surprised to find "that someone had suffered more than the son."[2] When we sin, we suffer consequences, and Someone suffers with us—and more deeply than we can suffer.

The more I have read and studied Hosea 11:8-9, the more impressed I have been with the depth of God's suffering with and for people. Through the prophet, He expressed His anguish over His people who were "determined to turn from" Him (v. 7). God said: "How can I give you up, Ephraim? How can I hand you over, Israel? . . . My heart is changed within me; all my compassion is aroused. I will not carry out my fierce anger, nor will I turn and devastate Ephraim. For I am God, and not man—the Holy One among you. I will not come in wrath" (vv. 8-9). God is pictured as

---

[1] J. Stanley Glen, *The Parables of Conflict in Luke* (Philadelphia: The Westminster Press, 1962), 31.
[2] Cargill, 30.

agonizing over His wayward people. Far from being detached, aloof, cold, uncaring, or vengeful, God is involved with people, yearns for them, and wants them to relate to Him redemptively.

The cross forever will stand as irrefutable evidence that God suffers with and for us. Our pain is His pain, but His pain is on a level we cannot approach.

Think for a moment about ways the father could have responded to the returning prodigal. He could have waited with arms folded across his chest and a stern frown on his face as his son hesitantly approached. The father could have turned and walked away, demonstrating his anger at and rejection of the son. The father could have unleashed a long string of "I told you so's" in anger. He could have delivered a scathing lecture outlining how the son had hurt the father and shamed the family. The father could have remained aloof and detached in a cool and reluctant reception. He could have demanded an apology while the son groveled at the father's feet. He could have received his son only on a probationary basis, making clear that the son would have to prove himself over an indefinite length of time. Leslie D. Weatherhead reported a Buddhist parallel to the meeting between a returning son and his father "which makes the father subject the boy on his return home to a long period of discipline, in order to prove his real repentance."[3] Malcolm O. Tolbert insightfully wrote: "The kind of homecoming a prodigal son can expect always depends on the kind of father he has to go back home to."[4] The prodigal in Jesus' story had the best kind of father waiting for him.

Keep in mind that at any point in the younger son's odyssey, the father could have disowned him—when the son walked away, during his stay in the far country, and when he approached the father with his confession and prepared request. The father could have run out of patience and could have written off his son. Yet in Jesus' story, to disown and write off the foolish and rebellious son was never an option. The father's actions give evidence that he never entertained the thought of giving up on his son.

The scene of the son's encounter with his father in Jesus' story is filled with indications of the father's warm and excited response. When the father saw his returning son, he "was filled with

---

[3] Weatherhead, *In Quest of a Kingdom* ,90.
[4] Tolbert, 126.

compassion" (v. 20b). The phrase translates one Greek word that conveys the idea of being moved with deep emotion. The noun form of the verb meant "the nobler viscera, that is, the heart, the lungs, the liver, and the intestines," which were held to be the seat of the emotions. [5] Metaphorically, it came to indicate "the heart, the affections of the heart, the tender affections."[6] Charles B. Williams translated the verb "moved with pity,"[7] its literal meaning. J. B. Phillips captured well the thrust of the word: "His heart went out to him."[8] In today's common expression, "He was deeply moved." The word Jesus used for the father's response to his returning son is the strongest Greek word for compassion.[9]

The father's compassion for his returning son well may be—and I am convinced is—the center or heart of the parable. Before the returning son could reach his father, and before he could begin his confession and request—before he could express repentance—the father's heart reached out for him. I. Howard Marshall wrote that the father's compassion "corresponds to the seeking and searching in the two preceding parables [in Luke 15]."[10]

Most of us may take for granted that God is compassionate. Many in New Testament times were not so sure or were convinced otherwise. William Barclay wrote: "Pagan religious thought believed in a God whose essence was that he was incapable of feeling pity. . . . The idea of a God who could be moved with compassion . . . must have come to such a world literally like a new revelation."[11] We know God is compassionate because Jesus said so. More than that, Jesus—God in human flesh—often was moved with compassion at people's plights (see Matt. 9:36; 14:14; 15:32; 20:34; Mark 1:41). His feeling *with* them issued in caring actions *for*

---

[5] William Barclay, *More New Testament Words* (New York: Harper & Row, Publishers, 1958), 156.
[6] *The Analytical Greek Lexicon* (New York: Harper & Row, Publishers, nd), 373.
[7] Charles B. Williams, *The New Testament in the Language of the People* (Nashville: Holman Bible Publishers, 1986), 171.
[8] Phillips, 159.
[9] Barclay, *More New Testament Words*, 159.
[10] I. Howard Marshall, "The Gospel of Luke: A Commentary on the Greek Text" in *The New International Greek Testament Commentary* (Grand Rapids, Michigan: William B. Eerdmans Publishing Company, 1978), 610.
[11] Barclay, *More New Testament Words*, 160.

The Compassionate Father

them. The major reason we can be confident that God is compassionate is Jesus' revelation of that amazing truth.

Even as in the incarnation Jesus put a human face on God's love and mercy, so He put a human face on God's compassion. Worth noting is the truth that compassion begins as the strong emotion of empathy but does not remain there. It moves beyond good intentions and high-sounding, proper religious words.to constructive action on others' behalf.

The Scriptures give us marvelous insights into God's character—not His total nature but more than enough to draw our commitment to Him. First Peter 5:6 assures believers they can put all their anxieties in God's hands because He *cares* for them. First John 4:8,16 state that God is *love*. In Luke 15:20 Jesus poignantly portrayed God as the God of *compassion*. Far from being aloof and unmoved by our plight, He is redemptively involved with us; He is with us and for us. The truth that God chooses to exercise His sovereign power in compassion is infinitely reassuring and encourages us to progressively deepen our commitment to Him.

The father in Jesus parable "ran to his son" (Luke 15:20b). In that day, Jewish men normally did not run in public; to do so was considered to be undignified. In his elation, the father cared nothing about dignity. He was not the least concerned with what other family members and workers on the farm thought of his demeanor. He caught up his returning son in a bear hug— "threw his arms around him and kissed him." Today, family members and good friends hug as an expression of affection and acceptance. On greeting and leaving, my daughter and my son—both of whom are young adults—share a hug with my wife and me as an expression of the love we share with one another. Among the most sought-after and treasured hugs are those of our grandsons and granddaughters. The shared warmth is a celebration of family ties.

The form of the Greek term rendered "kissed" in Jesus' story can convey repeated kissing or kissing tenderly. The Williams translation has "kissed him affectionately."[12] The Amplified New Testament reads "kissed him—fervently."[13] Clarence Jordan

---

[12] Williams, 171.
[13] *The Amplified New Testament* (Grand Rapids: Zondervan Publishing House, 1958), 275.

favored the translation "kissed him and kissed him."[14] The father's kiss has been viewed as an expression of forgiveness, reconciliation, and peace. To me, the father's kissing his son was an assurance of a love that had never been withdrawn. The father's actions were not expressions of good manners or matters of custom; they conveyed sincere, unqualified, open-armed welcome. The embrace and the kiss or kisses assured the son of His father's love and forgiveness before either spoke a word. This tender scene forever removes any doubt that the compassionate Heavenly Father will receive people who are burdened with guilt. Who can miss the human father's eagerness to hold the returning son next to his heart? How much more eager, then, is God to receive repentant sinners.

In the astonishing word image of the father who received his returning son with open arms, Jesus told His listeners—and us—truths about what God is like. The father's gathering the son in a bear hug and kissing his cheek warmly expresses the extension of grace—undeserved favor and acceptance. Note that in his desire to leave, the son staked his claim: "Give me my share of the estate" (v. 12). He demanded what was coming to him. The speech he rehearsed on his way back home acknowledged that he could make no demands on his father; nothing in him merited his father's favorable response to his planned request. He had no claim to make, only a plea for help. We have nothing on which to base any demand for God's acceptance, any claim to his favor. We only can ask, and He is more than ready to give grace.

The father's reception of his son expressed the element of mercy. Mercy can have the ideas of refusing to inflict pain on another person when one has the upper hand or of extending kindness when harshness is expected. The father certainly had all the power; the son had none. The son literally was at his father's mercy—and mercy is exactly what he received. God is like that. He has the power to punish or to extend incredible kindness. He chooses to extend kindness to people who approach Him in humility.

Jesus' clear point was that God openly, gladly, and warmly welcomes repentant sinners. What incredibly good news that is! No matter what we have done, God does not reject us. Neither does He receive us reluctantly, grudgingly. He does not beat us black

---

[14] Jordan, 62.

The Compassionate Father

and blue with our guilt. He does not angrily berate us for what we have done or withhold pardon until we prove ourselves. God imposes no probationary periods. He meets us with open arms and takes us to Himself.

The returning son began the carefully prepared, heartfelt speech he had rehearsed countless times on his way home. He confessed that he had sinned against God and against his father. With the words, "I am no longer worthy" (v. 21), He expressed his realization that he did not deserve to be his father's son. He only could ask to be received. That is as far as he got; he did not get to the part about being taken on as a hired servant. His father interrupted him.

Not all interpreters view the father's words to his servants as an interruption. John Nolland wrote that the plea, "Make me like one of your hired men," "would be to insult his father's love,"[15] so the appeal drops out of the text. I feel strongly that Jesus meant the father's words to be an interruption at the precise point the son expressed his unworthiness. Given his actions, he was not worthy. The broader truth is that no one is worthy. Sinners and tax collectors were well aware of being unworthy of God's grace. In His story, Jesus emphasized dramatically that God's receiving people is not a matter of worthiness but of God's unmerited, unstinting grace.

Think for a moment about the enormous amount of pride the returning prodigal had to swallow. Instead of coming home with outward trappings of success and a gloating "I-told-you-I-would-show-you" smile, he was in rags, with sunken cheeks and hollow eyes, wearing tattered clothing and barefoot. I can imagine he had trouble meeting his father's eyes. Gone now were the smug confidence and cocky swagger. Youthful pride had been replaced by a mark of hard-gained maturity—humility.

Evidently the returning prodigal either wanted to punish himself for what he had done or to have a chance to prove himself. Perhaps both motives lay behind his confession and planned request. J. Stanley Glen made an insightful suggestion about the prodigal's rehearsed request that his father take him in as a hired hand—a request he did not get to voice: "He could not conceive of returning to his father without imposing a penalty on himself as a

---

[15] Nolland, 785.

compensation for sin. His only thought was to demean himself to the lowest possible status."[16] Glen saw in the planned request a deep awareness of guilt. Also, the son had left home to gain freedom from what he viewed as the father's rules and restraints; he returned with the same erroneous understanding of his father, only to be met with unexpected grace.[17]

Words cannot describe the stunned surprise the prodigal no doubt experienced when his father received him warmly, cut short the son's planned request, and honored him. At worst, the returning prodigal expected to be rejected out of hand. At best, he hoped for an affirmative answer to his request to be a day laborer. Instead, he was surprised by love, mercy, and grace he could not comprehend. His so-called friends in the far country had deserted him; the people of that country had refused to help him. Yet a love that never had let him go enveloped him in its warmth. The father did more than the returning son expected. The God whom the father represented does far more than we have a right to expect. He loves us infinitely more than we can comprehend.

Only a casual or distracted reader can miss the excitement in the staccato directives the father gave his slaves in Jesus' story: "Quick! Bring the best robe . . . a ring . . . and sandals" (v. 22). His commands to his slaves made clear that he would spare no expense or effort to welcome his son back.

The robe was necessary to replace the tattered rags that inadequately clothed the son. The robe also symbolized honor and was provided for a special guest. It literally was "the first robe"— the finest robe in the closet. John Nolland has suggested that the words may indicate "'the former robe,' and thus the clothing that marked the son's place in the family before his departure."[18] The new clothing covered the son's body, but it also assured him of genuine, wholehearted reception.

Many commentators believe the ring was a signet ring that stood for authority. A contrasting view is that the ring was an expression of honor, not a signet ring, for "the son is . . . not made the plenipotentiary of his father."[19]

---

[16] Glen, 32.
[17] Ibid., 32-33.
[18] Nolland, 785.
[19] Ibid.

The Compassionate Father

Sandals probably were necessary because the son returned barefoot. Sandals also signified sonship in contrast to slavery. One of the songs slaves in America sang was "All God's Chillun Got a Song." Two of the verses proclaim: "I got shoes, you got shoes,/ All God's chillun got shoes;/ When I get to heab'n, goin' to put on my shoes,/ Goin' to walk all over God's heab'n./ I got a robe, you got a robe,/ All God's chillun got a robe;/ When I get to heab'n, goin' to put on my robe,/ Goin' to shout all over God's heab'n."[20] The slaves who sang this song knew they were God's children, and they longed for the time when that truth would be evident and they would enjoy the freedom that belonged to all members of God's family, not merely to slave owners. Their protest song was an affirmation of God's love for them.

Alfred Plummer felt that "none of the three things ordered are necessaries. The father is not merely supplying the wants of his son, who has returned in miserable and scanty clothing. He is doing him honour (sic)."[21] As has been pointed out, a contrasting view is that only the ring was not a necessity; the returning son needed clothes and shoes. All the items, however, conveyed the father's reception of the returning prodigal as a son. His being a day laborer was out of the question.

The father's actions in Jesus' story expressed pointedly his refusal to allow his son to be a hired servant, a day laborer. The father insisted that the young man be his son. George Arthur Buttrick suggested that the young man may have had mixed motives in planning to ask that he be taken on as a hired servant in his father's employ. "Perhaps it was escape. When a man is a slave [hired hand], he need make no decisions. What a relief! . . . The father in the parable waved aside the plea for servitude. 'This is my son' (vs. 24), he said. No man can escape responsibility, for every man is a son in his Father's house."[22] The robe, ring, and sandals marked the returning young man as a son with privileges *and* responsibilities.

The father restored the returning prodigal to a position of honor as his son. The son was granted the opportunity to begin again.

---

[20] J. Garfield Owens, *All God's Chillun: Meditations on Negro Spirituals* (Nashville: Abingdon Press, 1971), 13.
[21] Plummer, 376.
[22] Buttrick, "The Gospel According to St. Luke," 275.

One of the television pastors/preachers I enjoyed hearing had as the theme of his church's message, ministry, and television program that no matter who you are or what you have done, you can begin again—through God's grace. The father's insistence that the returning prodigal be restored to the honored position of son assures every sinner that he or she can begin again following God's forgiveness. The new beginning granted by grace carries corresponding demands that forgiven sinners live like God's children, bringing honor to Him.

"The fattened calf" (v. 23) was a calf kept in a stall and fed well in anticipation of a festive event—a special occasion that called for feasting. In that day, Jews seldom ate meat at meals. Jesus used the feature of the fattened calf to emphasize the special, festive quality of a person's coming home to God. The father instructed his slaves to prepare the best beef for a festive meal. A butchered calf probably would have supplied enough meat for scores of guests. Jesus used easily recognizable elements and customs of His time to stress God's joyous, lavish welcome of sinners who turn from their brokenness and turn to God's loving embrace.

Frank Stagg pointed out that "the father gave more than the son asked. He received him not as a hired servant but as a son. The father gave him not only clothing and a banquet, but first of all himself."[23] Think of it! When people approach God in humble confession and repentance, He accepts them and offers them Himself—His presence, love, and grace. Nothing in life is greater than the assurance that even though we are unacceptable, God loves and accepts us.

Some casual readers and even some serious Bible students have questions at this point in Jesus' story: Did not the returning son get off rather lightly? In his arrogance, selfishness, and wasteful and wild living, he deliberately had sinned against his father and against great love. He had shamed himself and had disgraced the family. The father did not even mention these evident truths. Instead, he welcomed the son with lavish gestures of acceptance and restoration to the family. Where is the comeuppance here? Where is penalty and punishment? Where is justice? No doubt, the Pharisees and the scribes who heard Jesus' words asked these questions silently.

---

[23] Stagg, 104.

The Compassionate Father

The father had no need to punish his son. The young man had punished himself, and he would continue to pay a tragically high price for what he had done. His descent into the pigs' sty was painfully humiliating. His coming to himself no doubt included a sharp realization of what he had done to his father (and in the background, to his mother). He always would live with the awareness of having sinned against great love. He saw what a mess he had made of his life. Approaching his father—with his hat in his hand, as it were—added to his humiliation. In addition, what was the son thinking as his father gave directives about a festive welcome? The contrast between forgiving love and self-willed rejection could not be presented more sharply. The livid scars of the son's far-country experience would remain as reminders of how costly sinning against love is. "Judgment is written across the story. The prodigal knew famine, shame that brought him as low as swine, loneliness—all the wretchedness of a soul alienated from man and God. There was no easy pardon!"[24]

Some readers have objected that the father's reception of his son was not natural. Few if any fathers would receive a returning prodigal in the manner Jesus described. That is the point exactly! "Not every father would respond as this father did to this set of circumstances, but Jesus' point is that the Heavenly Father always responds this way."[25] Not many human fathers forgive so completely and extend such unconditional love to children who deliberately have turned their backs on their fathers with such ingratitude, inflicting incredible pain on the parents, but God does—consistently.

Verse 24 presents the awfulness of separation from God and the glorious new beginning people experience in turning to Him. The father called the returning prodigal "this son of mine"—loved, valued, and now recovered. He described his son as having been "dead." The word could describe the father's bereavement because of his son's self-exile in the far country. To the father, the son had been as good as dead. Interestingly, the New Testament as a whole makes clear that separation from God is spiritual death (see Jas. 1:15; Rev. 20:14). The father in Jesus' story further described his

---

[24] Buttrick, "The Gospel According to St. Luke," 273.
[25] Robert J. Dean, "Luke" in *Layman's Bible Book Commentary*, vol. 17 (Nashville: Broadman Press, 1983), 100.

son as having been "lost" (Luke 15:24). The young man had been lost to himself and to his father. He had been lost in the sense of not being able to find his way in a sometimes harsh and demanding world but also in the sense of being self-exiled from home. The words "dead" and "lost" express the great peril in which the younger son had placed himself by distancing himself from his father. The son had not merely fallen on hard times; he had endangered his life.

The contrast created by the son's return is striking: The young man now was "alive" in a way he had not been before, and he was "found." After the father's lengthy time of fearful and anxious waiting, the prodigal had come back home. His arrival called for the whole household to "have a feast and celebrate" (v. 23). Literally, the father said: "Having eaten, let us be glad." In that time as in ours, meals were events designed to mark special occasions. All members of the household, including slaves, were invited to the feast. This event called for unbridled rejoicing.

Jesus used a brilliant color in His last brush stroke in the vivid scene of the father's welcoming his son home: "They began to celebrate" (v. 24)—or as Clarence Jordan translated, "They began to whoop it up."[26] The Greek word translated "celebrate" was used in verse 23 and means "to be glad," "to be merry," "to rejoice." It has the idea of feasting in an expression of joy. It occurs again in verses 29 and 32. Jesus was teaching that God leads in celebration when people come home to Him, His love, and His grace.

In the two previous parables in Luke 15, the note of joy at finding something lost is pronounced. The shepherd who found the one lost sheep called his friends and neighbors together and asked them to rejoice with him (v. 6). The woman who found her lost coin after a thorough (and no doubt frantic) search of her house gathered her friends and neighbors and invited them to rejoice with her (v. 9). In both instances, Jesus stressed that rejoicing takes place "in heaven" and "in the presence of the angels of God" when "one sinner . . . repents" (vv. 7,10). These are ways of expressing the truth that God celebrates when people turn to Him. The terms "heaven" and "the angels of God" were oblique

---

[26] Jordan, 62.

The Compassionate Father

ways of referring to God and reflect the Jews' reluctance to use God's name directly because of their deep reverence for it.

Years ago, I preached a sermon titled "When God Laughs" based on Luke 15:8-10. I was convinced then and remain convinced that when a person comes home to God's great love—when he or she experiences God's compassion—God's booming laugh of pure pleasure reverberates through heaven as it were, inviting all heaven's residents to join Him in celebration. The image may be somewhat crude, but I think God responds to repentant sinners in a manner somewhat analogous to but infinitely greater than our joyous laughter.

In Jesus' scene of the prodigal's return, we see ourselves in the young man. George A. Buttrick asked, "Who, then, is the *'prodigal'* in this story? Anybody given over to gross fleshliness? Yes, and the whole race of men besides—a planet living for externals, and acting the primeval lie of 'self-expression.' "[27] No matter whether our motives for turning to God are mixed, He will receive us, will use our coming as a starting point for us, and will continue to move us toward maturity as His sons and daughters. He has infinite compassion and welcomes us to Himself. He does not hold over us what we have done; we do not have to live in fear of repeated recriminations. He forgives us and grants us a new start.

Again, we also see clearly in the scene that none of us deserves to be included in God's family. We all have sinned and have come woefully short of God's standards (see Rom. 3:23). We have nothing with which to negotiate God's reception of us. In addition, no matter how morally good, intelligent, talented, or religious we might view ourselves to be, we cannot lay claim to relationship with God on our merits. He receives us out of sheer grace and unbelievable love when we place our faith in Christ and accept the salvation He has provided. Only God's great compassion for us makes possible our being forgiven.

For us to approach God in repentance requires the death of pride. We must abandon self-reliance for redemption and cast ourselves on God's mercy. In the area of salvation, we are not capable of "doing it ourselves"; we must receive the Heavenly Father's grace.

---

[27] Buttrick, *The Parables of Jesus*, 194.

We learn from Jesus' words that God loves us with a love that defies our understanding. God is not a stern, glowering deity. He is not angry, bitter, or vindictive toward us because of our sins against Him. The great heart of God is filled with love and compassion for us; His arms are open wide to receive us. The father's reception of his returning son is about God's incredible, astonishing love.

We should be eternally grateful that no matter how far we remove ourselves from God in rebellion against Him, He never gives up on us; He never lets us go. Some human fathers may lose patience and leave wayward children to their own devices, but God never does. His infinite patience awaits the slightest movement toward Him and home. In that instant He is there, arms spread wide in loving welcome. The warmth of His smile assures us of an infinite kindness beyond our imagining.

The father's actions toward the son reveal that God insists on our being responsible members of His family. To be sure, in a real sense we are his servants. In the Old Testament, to be God's servant was an honor. Paul referred to himself as "a servant [*doulos*, bond slave] of Christ Jesus" (Rom. 1:1) and "a servant [*doulos*, bond slave] of God" (Titus 1:1). To be related to God is to be His slave. The startling paradox is that only as His slaves do we experience true freedom; real freedom is found in obedient service for Him. Yet more than slaves, we are Christ's friends. In John 15:14-15, Jesus said to His disciples: "You are my friends if you do what I command. I no longer call you servants, because a servant does not know his master's business. Instead, I have called you friends." James wrote that "Abraham . . . was called God's friend" (Jas. 2:23). Moreover, people who have placed their faith in Christ are God's children—sons and daughters in His family. In 1 John 3:1, John wrote: "How great is the love the Father has lavished on us, that we should be called children of God! And that is what we are!" The terms *slave, friend,* and *child* describe different dimensions of a rich relationship that involves responsibilities of obedience, faithfulness, and growth toward spiritual maturity. God insists that we not be automatons who have our every move dictated but that we live as children who act in ways that reflect well on Him and His family of faith.

A decided emphasis in Jesus' word picture in Luke 15:24 is that sin issues in death and lostness. Sin sometimes can and does lead to physical death, but it always results in spiritual death if people refuse to repent and place their faith in Christ. Paul wrote: "The wages of sin is death, but the gift of God is eternal life in Christ Jesus our Lord" (Rom. 6:23). God offers the gift of life to all people, no matter who they are and what they have done. To be separated from God is to be lost. When we are alienated from God, we are lost to Him, to others, and to ourselves. Whether people carelessly wander away from God or deliberately reject Him, they are lost and need to be found by God's love that He goes on extending to them. Turning to God is turning to home.

Jesus revealed a delightful truth about God in the scene of homecoming He painted—a truth that is difficult to express adequately: God is absolutely delighted when people come home to Him. An incredible truth in the words "they began to celebrate" (Luke 15:24) is that God is elated when people come home to Him. Actually, our vocabulary is far too meager and poor to describe God's response when people approach Him in repentance. To state that He is happy, rejoices, is overjoyed, is ecstatic, is elated, or is pleased does not begin to capture the depth of His response. His greatest satisfaction, I am convinced, is to welcome another sinner home.

In our day, many parents have agonized over children who have been sucked into the sewer of drug addiction and/or alcoholism. These children literally have left home or they have rejected the high values that parents tried to instill. When these children come to themselves and turn their lives around, parents experience joy beyond description. Their experience is a dim reflection of God's response when people turn to Him for forgiveness. His greatest pleasure is reclaiming people who had been lost to Him.

In the father's lavish reception of his son, Jesus stressed God's unimaginable graciousness and generosity toward people who come home to Him. Paul was fond of pointing out God's liberality toward us. In Romans 2:4, he alluded to "the riches of his [God's] kindness." In Ephesians 1:7-8, He wrote: "In him [Christ] we have redemption through his blood, the forgiveness of sins, in accordance with the riches of God's grace that he lavished on us with all wisdom and understanding." In Ephesians 2:4, he stated: "Because of his great love for us, God, who is rich in mercy, made us alive with Christ even when we were dead in transgressions." In Ephesians 2:7 he referred to "the incomparable riches of his [God's] grace, expressed in his kindness to us in Christ Jesus." Paul assured the Philippian Christians: "My God will meet all your needs according to his glorious riches in Christ Jesus" (Phil. 4:19). God gives more than we can imagine—and infinitely more than we deserve.

Years ago, I read the book *Surprised by Joy*—C. S. Lewis's account of his journey from atheism to commitment to Christ. The book's title states a marvelous truth for every person who has come to Christ for salvation; all believers have experienced a surprising, lasting joy—a deep confidence of being held securely in God's everlasting arms. As in the case of the returning younger son in Jesus' story, people who have placed their faith in Christ have been surprised by incredible grace, love, and compassion. The hymn writer stated beautifully an amazing truth: "There's a wideness in God's mercy, / Like the wideness of the sea. . . . / But we make his love too narrow/ By false limits of our own;/ And we magnify his strictness/ With a zeal he will not own. / For the love of God is broader/ Than the measure of one's mind;/ And the heart of the Eternal/ Is most wonderfully kind."[28]

Reflected in the father's instructions to his slaves to prepare a sumptuous banquet is the truth that continued relationship with God can be compared with a celebration—a banquet or a feast. Life with God is meant to be marked by joy (not to be confused with happiness, which depends on circumstances)—a deep and abiding assurance of His love and care. In commenting on another parable of Jesus, Leslie D. Weatherhead wrote: "The man who has not received from his religion something that is comparable with a feast, something that is joyous and radiant and glad, has not yet got what is offered."[29] When God receives us, we enter a relationship marked by ongoing celebration of His grace and goodness.

During His ministry, Jesus referred to the Messianic banquet at the end of the age. In Luke 13:28, He warned people who rejected Him that they would weep and grind their teeth when they saw Abraham, Isaac, Jacob, and the prophets in the kingdom of God and realized that the outsiders had excluded themselves. Then Jesus said: "People will come from east and west and north and south, and will take their places at the feast in the kingdom of God" (v.

---

[28] Frederick W. Faber, "There's a Wideness in God's Mercy" (No. 25, *The Baptist Hymnal*, 1991)
[29] Weatherhead, *In Quest of a Kingdom*, 113.

29). In the life hereafter with God, all people who receive Christ as Savior will be present at the Messianic banquet. Of significance is that life with God, here and now and in the future, is presented in terms of a feast—a joyous celebration. The celebration that begins with a sinner's salvation will continue through eternity. The good news is that everybody can join the party through faith in Christ.

Scene 5: A Plea of Impartial Love (VV. 25-32)

25 *"Meanwhile, the older son was in the field. When he came near the house, he heard music and dancing.* **26** *So he called one of the servants and asked him what was going on.* **27** *'Your brother has come,' he replied, 'and your father has killed the fattened calf because he has him back safe and sound.'* **28** *The older brother became angry and refused to go in. So, his father went out and pleaded with him.* **29** *But he answered his father, 'Look! All these years I've been slaving for you and never disobeyed your orders. Yet you never gave me even a young goat so I could celebrate with my friends.* **30** *But when this son of yours who has squandered your property with prostitutes comes home, you kill the fattened calf for him!'* **31** *'My son,' the father said, 'you are always with me, and everything I have is yours.* **32** *But we had to celebrate and be glad, because this brother of yours was dead and is alive again; he was lost and is found.'"*

The Compassionate Father

The final scene Jesus painted in His mural has dark, somber hues—the same colors He used in Scene 2 to depict the prodigal's plight. The shades and tones in Scene 5 contrast sharply with the bright colors of the prodigal's return. Only the father's tender, loving entreaties and patient reasoning with his older son relieve the tension and conflict. The older son's anger, hostility, and accusation color the scene in harsh tones that are broken only by the father's obvious compassion for his older son.

At one time, some scholars contended that Jesus' parable originally ended with verse 24: the celebration of the prodigal's return. They believed verses 25-32 were an addition or appendix. Today, this view has largely been rejected. I agree with interpreters who consider verses 11-32 to be a unity. Verses 25-32 are not merely an afterthought. Jesus clearly indicated as much with his opening words of the story in verse 1: "There was a man who had *two* sons" (italics mine). Both sons were integral to the parable; they were vital to the message Jesus wanted to convey to tax collectors and sinners and to the religious leaders who rejected them and opposed Him.

The prodigal had returned, the father had welcomed him home, and the merrymaking was under way. The father, everyone connected with his household, and perhaps invited guests were enjoying the festivities that celebrated the prodigal's return—with one exception. The older son was working "in the field" (v. 25). To this point, Jesus had not referred directly to the older brother; the Lord had said that a father had two sons. Then He had focused on the younger son and the father. Now the spotlight falls on the father and his older son.

In my mind's eye, I can see the older brother as he calls it a day and prepares to head toward home. Dusk is deepening toward darkness. The older son gathers his implements and begins the long walk from the field to the house. He has done another long day's work alongside his father's slaves, whom he supervised. He feels satisfaction at what he has accomplished. He experiences the pleasant tiredness of having put in a good day's labor. As he approaches the house, he becomes aware of unusual activity. Every lamp in the house must be lighted, for he can see the glow from a distance. As he draws closer, he hears the sound of music, clapping, and people dancing. The slight breeze carries the mouthwatering aroma of cooked meat. What in the world can be going on?

Two things immediately stand out in the introduction of the older brother. The first factor is that the father had gone to great lengths to provide everything needed for the festive occasion that marked the younger son's return. The Greek word translated "music" is the term from which we get our word *symphony*. The father had hired musicians—perhaps flute players—to play. Their music probably was accompanied by handclapping and singing. The men were dancing to the music. The Greek term translated "dancing"—*choros*—forms part of our word *choreography*. "*[Choros]* is the choral dance with gestures, clapping of hands, perhaps also steps and is done by chosen performers as a spectacle for the audience."[1] The dancing also may have been accompanied by choral singing. The father well may have engaged a group of dancers for the occasion. Jesus painted a scene marked by music, gaiety, and laughter.

The second element in the introduction of the older brother is a positive characteristic he displayed: He was industrious and dependable. During the younger brother's absence, the older son had continued to work hard and consistently. He may have done so partly because he had a vested interest in the land; for all intents and purposes, it all was his now. More likely, he did so because he was a hard worker. He was a conscientious, reliable son who faithfully discharged his responsibilities.

Notice that in many respects, the older brother was not a patently bad man. In fact, he probably was a good man, a solid citizen. He had not wasted his father's money—or his own. He may have been staid, stuffy, and lacking in personality, but he performed his tasks well. He did not shirk his duties, and he worked alongside his father. Again, this indicates that he was part of a wealthy family with land holdings large enough that he and probably his father both supervised other workers and worked along side them. The older son had remained at home and was fulfilling the Commandment to honor (take care of) his parents. To this point, he had been a good, dependable son. He was loyal and responsible.

Rather than continue his walk home, the older brother stopped and inquired about the festivities (v. 26). He called one of the

---

[1] Lenski, 818.

paidon, either a slave or a hired servant. The Greek term may indicate a boy, or it can be used as "boy" in the sense of a servant. The older brother asked what the merrymaking meant. The tense of the Greek verb rendered "asked" conveys repeated inquiry—he kept on asking, pressing for an answer. In the servant's reply, Jesus introduced one of the emphases of this final scene in His mural: "*Your brother* has come" (v. 27, italics mine). I can only imagine the stunning force with which these words struck the older brother. He could not have been more shocked had the servant slapped him. Likely, the older son had written off his younger brother and had not missed him. He probably had dismissed from thought the family's black sheep. In fact, things probably had gone smoothly in the prodigal's absence, even if the younger son had not been present to share the work. As far as the elder brother was concerned, his brother's leaving and continued absence had been good riddance. No evidence is given that he had shared his father's grief and anxiety concerning the younger son's welfare in the far country. That he did not drop his tools and sprint to the house to embrace his brother stands out and speaks volumes.

The news of the younger brother's arrival continued with words that struck the elder brother like repeated hammer blows. Instead of receiving the cold shoulder or outright rejection from his father, the prodigal was the honored guest at a feast! Of all things, the father had slaughtered the "fattened calf" (v. 27) and was presiding at a banquet!

In Jesus' story, the servant's words that express the reason for the father's lavish display of relief and joy at the prodigal's return were designed to penetrate the formidable defenses of the religious leaders in Jesus' audience. The father led in the celebration because he had his younger son "back safe and sound." Literally, the Greek text reads: "because he recovered him [received him back] being in health" (v. 27). Given the younger son's harrowing experience, he was in reasonably good shape physically. Yet he experienced recovery on a much deeper level. Robert H. Stein wrote, "'Safe and sound' is literally *healthy*. More is implied than his physical health. In the picture part of the parable this would refer to his moral and spiritual health; but in the reality part, to his having received salvation."[2] Salvation is recovery on life's deepest level. Jesus' point

---

[2] Stein, 407.

on a spiritual level was that God had recovered sinners and tax collectors who had been lost to Him, and He took great delight in that.

Jesus' next words rang like the sudden, sharp reverberation of a thunder clap: "The older brother became angry" (v. 28). That translation does not do justice to the force of Jesus' word choice. The Greek word rendered "angry" is *orgisthe:* "He was enraged." J. B. Phillips translated the words, "He was furious."[3] Clarence Jordan colorfully rendered the Greek term as "He blew his top."[4] The noun *orge* has the idea of a settled, seething resentment. It is the same word used of God's wrath—His settled opposition to sin (see Rom. 1:18). Another Greek term, *thumos,* literally means "to rush along," "to be in heat," "to breathe violently." It conveys anger that flares up quickly and burns brightly, much as straw set ablaze; then it dies out. The older brother's deep, simmering resentment boiled to the surface when he learned that his good-for-nothing brother had returned to a warm welcome from his father. Jesus drew a sharp, startling contrast between the father's forgiving love and compassion (Luke 15:20) and the older brother's explosive anger and deep-seated resentment. Did the religious leaders feel the full impact of Jesus' words? Did they "get it"?

For all the older brother's good qualities, he had a serious sin problem. The younger brother's sins were visible and well documented. The older brother's sin of attitude was subtler but no less serious.

The implication of Jesus' words is that the older brother's rage was long-standing. Had he resented his younger brother long before the prodigal had left home? Some interpreters conjecture that the younger boy—for all his impetuousness, insensitivity, and ingratitude—had a winsomeness, an attractiveness, that the older brother lacked. The younger brother well may have been personable and fun loving, while the older brother may have been straight-laced—a no-nonsense kind of guy. Whatever the case, the older brother evidently had nurtured a carefully pent-up rage against his brother that now spilled out into the open.

Jesus applied a darkly ominous brush stroke to His extensive mural: "The older brother . . . refused to go in" (v. 28). Literally, he

---

[3] Phillips, 160.
[4] Jordan, 62.

"was not willing to enter." The tense of the Greek verb conveys the idea of continuing unwillingness to enter the house, of steady resistance. The father wanted to include the older son in the celebration, but he stubbornly chose to exclude himself.

The son, seething outside the house, refused to fulfill his role as elder son in the celebration. Refusing to eat with the rest of the family was a serious breach of custom, for family bonds were strengthened by eating together. The prodigal had been lost to his father but had come home; the older brother also was lost to his father. As various interpreters have noted, he was the prodigal who stayed at home.

Jesus made two emphatic points here. First, as noted earlier, salvation is celebration, and God invites all people to join the party. Second, if anyone is excluded, he or she is self-excluded; the person chooses not to attend the party. To choose not to take part is to miss out on life as celebration in fellowship with the Father and with other members of His family.

Jesus must have looked at the Pharisees and the scribes with love and longing as He continued His story: "So his father went out and pleaded with him" (v. 28). Evidently, someone had told the father that his older son was outside, angrily refusing to join the party. As the father had run to meet the returning prodigal, so now he went out to urge his older son to join the festivities. The Greek word translated "pleaded" conveys continuing action in past time: "was pleading." The term can be rendered "was begging," "was entreating," "was imploring." Over and over, the father tried to reach his older son with the same love he was demonstrating toward the returning prodigal. Although the word *compassion* is not used, the father's entreaty displayed this consistent quality of his character. In the father's actions and words, Jesus was saying to the religious leaders, "Come to my table. Join the rest of the family. My table also has room for you." Note that one problem the religious leaders had with Jesus was His enjoying table fellowship with tax collectors and sinners (v. 2). Toward the end of his parable, He invited the religious leaders to join fellowship with the God who valued them and every other person—and with all other members of God's family. The good news for us is that God loves every person, and He extends to everybody His invitation to receive His grace.

The older son countered his father's pleas with sharp, angry words. "Look here!" he said roughly. "For these many years I continue to slave for you and never [not even once] have I disregarded your command" (v. 29, my paraphrase). Even as the prodigal had not understood the meaning of sonship, the older brother also had missed it. Note that he saw his relationship with his father in terms of slavery, drudgery, and toil. He worked hard, but to him it was performance of joyless duty. Helmut Thielicke noted that "there are no festivals in this life, but only tedious, tiresome, though highly serious, monotony."[5] Also, the older son viewed his years of labor as a bargaining chip to be used with his father at a time when it was needed. He drew a sharp contrast between his loyalty and the younger son's wantonness. In addition, the older son was self-righteous; he had followed orders without fail, and it was a point of pride with him. He had remained at home, but he had created his own far country. He "was in one sense a good man; but his goodness was hard, grim, self-righteous, critical, and unlovely, because he had none of the father's love in his heart."[6]

Note the implied truth Jesus was trying to drive home to the religious leaders. The prodigal had swallowed his pride and had approached his father in humble repentance. Publicans and sinners humbly and gladly had accepted God's invitation to celebration. The Pharisees and the scribes continued to allow their pride in their religious pedigrees and accomplishments and their smug sense of superiority to be a barrier to fellowship with the Father and with other people. They scrupulously kept God's commands; they had not transgressed as had the publicans and sinners. No doubt the Pharisee in Jesus' story in Luke 18:9-14 was not the only religious leader to remind God of his righteousness. I feel Jesus deliberately drew the sharp contrast between the prodigal's confession "I have sinned" and his acknowledgment "I am no longer worthy to be called your son" (15: 21) and the older brother's proud assertion in verse 29: "All these years I've . . . never disobeyed your orders."

An interesting question arises at this point: How did the older son view his father? The son's declaration that he had slaved for his father and always had obeyed his orders gives the impression the

---

[5] Thielicke, 33.
[6] Barclay, *And Jesus Said*, 180.

son considered his father to be demanding and exacting. Seemingly, he had little if any comprehension of his father's love for him. The older son's words well may have emphasized the religious leaders' view of their relationship with God. They slavishly kept the law and held up to public view their obedience to all His commands. In reality, God wanted willing service for Him in love; they had forged chains of legalism, bonds of dry-as-dust duty.

The older son followed heated, self-serving words with an accusation: "You never [not even once] gave me a goat in order that I might feast with my friends" (v. 29, literal translation). A goat would have cost about a denarius, a laborer's daily wage. For the father to give the older son a goat to be served at a feast would have been inexpensive. Note the words "that I might feast with *my friends*" (italics mine). Amazingly, the older brother "does not see that he is exhibiting much the same spirit as his brother. He wants to have his father's property in order that he may enjoy himself *apart from* [the father]."[7] Had the older son ever asked for a goat so he could throw a party? I also wonder how many "friends" would have accepted an invitation to his feast. Perhaps some would have come merely for the food. What would a party hosted by the stuffy older brother have been like?

What seeps through the older brother's anger-filled, almost whining words are jealousy and self-pity. Did he feel that his father had taken him for granted? John Nolland wrote that "it is not a goat as such that he wants . . . but recognition. . . . From the elder son's point of view, his father had made the prodigal not only equal but superior."[8] Were the Pharisees and the scribes jealous and angry because Jesus was attentive to tax collectors and sinners rather than courting the favor of the religious elite?

Today, reliable, obedient children often do not get the attention parents frequently give problem children. Children who give parents no trouble can feel that they have become part of the familiar family landscape and largely are taken for granted. Many times, the result is resentment and anger. The older son deeply resented his brother and was angry with his father. Yet the parable

---

[7] Plummer, 378.
[8] Nolland, 787.

indicates clearly that the father did not short-change his older son (see v. 12).

J. Stanley Glen wrote: "What makes the situation worse and acutely offensive is that [the prodigal] is to be allowed to live off the portion of the estate that rightly belongs to [the] elder brother."[9] Though technically this may be correct, I prefer to think that because the father was entitled to live off the proceeds of the estate, he planned to share his living with his younger son. The older son still would receive the entire estate as his inheritance. "It was doubtless the intention of Jesus . . . to indicate . . . how the grace of God is always offensive to those who insist on justice and nothing more."[10]

The older brother sharply contrasted his hard-working loyalty and filial obedience to his brother's character and actions. By doing so, he continued to distance himself from the prodigal. He first had done so by refusing to go in to the banquet and to welcome his brother. The older son called his younger brother "this son of yours" (v. 30). Notice: He did not say "my brother." In fact, he was saying, "He is no brother of mine." The words drip with sarcasm and must have cut the father like a knife. The older son also blamed his father for having such a son as the prodigal. In essence, he rebuked his father. The older brother described his brother as the one who "squandered" the father's living or "property." The Greek word translated "squandered" means "devoured," "consumed," "ate up." The son now eating the food the father had provided for the banquet—"the fattened calf" (v. 30)—already had consumed his portion of the goods the father had accumulated. The older son's words dripped with irony. The contrast he drew between the "young goat" (v. 29) and "the fattened calf" (v. 30) accentuated his anger. In the older son's mind, His father would not spend one denarius for him, but he would spare no effort or expense for the younger, sorry excuse for a son.

In angrily reminding his father that the younger son had wasted part of the family estate, "the older brother is not forgetting the distribution of V 12: he thinks in terms of the accumulated wealth the father had husbanded, which was designed to be the basis of

---

[9] Glen, 34.
[10] Ibid., 34.

livelihood for the family from generation to generation. The younger son had broken the chain and squandered what had been (part of) his father's livelihood and should have been kept intact for his own livelihood and that of his own sons in turn."[11] His concern for his inheritance left no room for concern for his brother. Forgiveness was out of the question; he would not willingly share anything with the prodigal, and he certainly would not celebrate his brother's recovery.

The older son accused his younger brother of spending the father's money "with prostitutes." Interestingly, the earlier description of the prodigal's wastefulness did not specify that he spent money on prostitutes. He had engaged in "wild living" (v.13)—living unsavingly (extravagantly). He had been a spendthrift, but nothing indicates he had engaged in immoral conduct. He well may have done so, for such conduct was common in Gentile lands; but the older brother would have had no way to know *how* his brother had thrown away his money. The older brother evidently assumed that the prodigal had been with prostitutes, so the older son harshly condemned his brother. Some interpreters have wondered whether the older brother's accusation reflected what he would have done—what he would like to have done—if he had been in the far country to which his brother had gone. With his pockets stuffed with money and in a place where no one knew him, perhaps the older brother would have done some wild living himself.

The older son lacked compassion. He was self-righteous, judgmental, and hard-hearted. Worst of all, "there was no love in the elder brother's creed. . . . He had not felt his brother's suffering in a far country or ever shared the father's grief."[12] The older brother—the other prodigal—never left home. His body was at home, but he never was at home in spirit, in attitude, or in proper relationship with his father.

Behind the words "you kill the fattened calf for him" (v. 30) was the older son's protest that the father was not fair. The older son was incredulous at what had transpired. We can almost hear him: "You killed the fattened calf *for him?* For that undeserving, pathetic

---

[11] Nolland, 787.
[12] Buttrick, "The Gospel According to St. Luke," 280.

parody of a son?" In fact, the older son accused the father of being partial.

I confess that for a long time, I had difficulty with this part of Jesus' story. I am well aware that in some families with more than one child, parents select a chosen child. Jacob was not the only father to select a favorite child, and Joseph was not the first or last child to take advantage of such an unwise choice (see Gen. 37:3,5-11). Even people who were not their parents' favorites make the tragic mistake of selecting a favorite child. Jacob should have known better. His father Isaac favored Esau, while Jacob's mother Rebekah favored Jacob (see Gen. 25:28). A severe conflict issued from those choices. On the surface, the father in Jesus' story could be charged with going overboard in his treatment of the returning prodigal and negligent where the older son was concerned.

Partiality, however, is not a factor in the drama of the father and his two sons. Remember that in the beginning of the story, the father divided his living between his two sons. The older son received two-thirds of the estate. The father was fair with both sons. Perhaps part of the older son's problem with his brother's return was that the younger son would live off the estate even though he had thrown away his portion. Yet remember that the entire estate actually belonged to the older son. He would inherit everything.

Part of the older son's problem was with his father. Instead of making the prodigal pay for his mistakes, the father seemed to act as though what the younger son had done did not matter. To the older son, the father's allowing the prodigal to come back home was a terrible mistake; worse yet was the father's not penalizing the wasteful young man. The creed by which the older brother lived called for justice; it had no place for grace, mercy, or love.

The older brother's most apparent problem was his relationship—actually, lack of relationship—with his brother. He felt no responsibility for his brother and condemned him out of hand. The deeper problem, however, was his relationship with his father. In his thinking, his father was operating off a wrong set of standards. The older son sought to set his father straight. The older son's attitude toward his father indicated a chasm as wide as that between the prodigal and his father when the younger son was in the far country. If the younger son had insulted his father by asking for his part of the inheritance and then leaving home, the older brother insulted his father by refusing to join the family in celebration, by deliberately failing to address his father as father, by rejecting his brother, and by his angry accusations against his father. Also, he dishonored his father by causing him to leave his duties as host to go out to his sulking son. With vivid strokes, Jesus painted the reality of both sons' sins against their father.

The older brother's heated words and caustic attitude cast a pall over the festivities taking place inside the house. His protests and vindictiveness affected his father, who wanted both his sons to be related properly to him. Such behavior would affect the younger son, who no doubt already felt guilty about what he had done to his family and about leaving the older brother to discharge the work responsibilities while the prodigal lived the high life in the far country. The older brother's refusal to take part in the welcoming feast cast the proverbial wet blanket over the celebration. Jesus wanted the religious leaders to comprehend the effects of their refusing to accept people such as tax collectors and sinners.

Jesus wanted the Pharisees and the scribes to see their two-pronged crisis: their rejection of the tax collectors and sinners—their brothers—and their view that God was unjust in receiving people who were not righteous, good, or religious. The barrier that separated the tax collectors and sinners from God was their sins; the barrier that separated the religious leaders from God was their self-perceived goodness. Because they considered themselves to be good, they looked down on others they deemed to be irreligious and felt that God was obligated to the religious leaders. They expected Him to adhere to their standards. Jesus' words were a rebuke to the religious leaders, but it was a gentle rebuke designed to draw positive response.

The father in Jesus' story heard his older son out and met the son's angry accusations and insinuations with tenderness. His opening words, "my son" (v. 31) reflect a reminder: "You are also my valued son." The Greek word for "son" is *teknon*, "a much more endearing term than *uios*, which is the usual word for **son**."[13] Charles B. Williams translated the Greek term *teknon* as "child,"[14] which captures the warmth the father intended. The father reached out to his older son with the same compassion he felt for the

---

[13] Ibid., 279.
[14] Williams, 172.

returning prodigal. With infinite patience and gentleness, the father reminded his older son that the son was always with him. I get the feeling that behind the father's reminder was a gentle question: "Don't you know me by now?" Had not the older son experienced the father's love and provision? Had not the son noticed how his father related to and treated other people and him? Had not the father always treated his son more than fairly? Why should what was happening now be a surprise? Jesus was emphasizing that God valued the religious leaders as much as He did the tax collectors and sinners and reached out to the Pharisees and scribes with the same love and compassion. The religious leaders might exclude other people, but God did not exclude the leaders. They could, however, exclude themselves.

Then the father said to his disgruntled, enraged son, "Everything I have is yours." In Jesus' story, the statement was true literally. Technically, following the division of the property and the younger son's converting his part of the estate into cash, the older brother owned everything. He had access to the father's wealth. In reality, the older son did not have to ask for a goat to slaughter and serve at a feast; he had at hand the resources he needed.

Jesus was reminding the religious leaders of God's provision for them. God was Israel's Father who had freed the people from slavery and had provided for them during the wilderness wanderings. He had made a covenant with them and had given them the Ten Words as guidelines for their living. He had given them a land and had remained faithful to them in spite of their unfaithfulness to Him. The Israelites had God's revelation through the prophets, the psalmists, and the wisdom writers. They really did not understand, however, what being God's children meant. The religious leaders of Jesus' day no doubt loved the Law, but they viewed their relationship with God in terms of rigid legalism that they felt earned righteousness for them. They were so busy working hard to keep all the rules they had formulated that they had no time to enjoy the Father's grace and love. Theirs was a joyless religion that shut out many people and reflected a distorted understanding of God.

The father in Jesus' story explained to his older son, "We *had to* celebrate and be glad" (v. 32, italics mine). The words "had to" translate the Greek term *edei*, which literally is "it was necessary." The word conveys the idea of moral necessity. The father did not apologize for his actions but spoke in gentle reproach, saying in essence, "You ought to be glad and make merry, since it is *your* brother who has come home."[15] "The welcome to the younger son was not simply a good thing which might or might not have occurred. It was the right thing. The father had to do it. Joy was the only proper reaction in such a situation."[16] Norval Geldenhuys suggested that "celebrate" *(euphranthenai)* reflected outward rejoicing and "be glad" *(carina)* indicated inward joy.[17] Relief and elation created by the prodigal's return had to be expressed. Most of us have no trouble identifying with the father's strong statement. We have experienced joy that had to be expressed verbally or physically. The younger son's return generated unbridled gladness. In the far country, he had been as good as dead, but now he had new life; he had been lost to himself and to his father, but now he had been recovered.

The older brother had referred to the prodigal as "this son of yours" (v. 30), a sneering, emphatic denial of relationship with the younger brother and a slap in his father's face. As we have seen, the force of the words may have been, "You are to blame for having such a son." In verse 32, the father gently but firmly stressed the relationship the older son denied, calling the younger son "this brother of yours." The father had refused to let the prodigal be less than a son (v. 22); he would not let the prodigal who had stayed at home be less than a brother. In effect, the father was saying, "If I have gained a son, thou hast gained a brother."[18] As Malcolm O. Tolbert wrote concerning Jesus' parable, "The whole problem is one of relationships—the relationship of a father to two sons, of the sons to the father, and of the sons to each other."[19]

Worth noting is the father's implied emphasis that the celebration over the prodigal's return would go on in spite of the older brother's protests. Jesus was stressing to the religious leaders that

---

[15] Jeremias, *The Parables of Jesus*, 131.
[16] Leon Morris, "The Gospel According to St. Luke" in *Tyndale Bible Commentaries* (Grand Rapids, Michigan: William B. Eerdmans Publishing Company, 1974), 244.
[17] Norval Geldenhuys, "Commentary on the Gospel of Luke" in *The New International Commentary on the New Testament* (Grand Rapids, Michigan: Wm. B. Eerdmans Publishing Company, 1960), 413.
[18] Plummer, 379.
[19] Tolbert, 125.

God's receiving all people who responded positively to His revelation of Himself in Christ would not be canceled because of the religious leaders' protests and resistance. Jesus would continue His ministry of seeking and saving the lost (see Luke 19:10).

The story closes with the father's attempt to get his older son to see the magnitude of the younger brother's return. The father used the same words he had spoken in directing his servants to prepare to celebrate (v. 24). The repetition emphasizes the significance of people's salvation. Yet a question forever will remain unanswered: Did the older brother go into the feast? Did he respond positively to his father's appeals and accept his brother?

In the final scene in Jesus' dramatic mural, can we summon the courage and honesty to see ourselves in the older brother? He is so unattractive, unyielding, and vindictive that we recoil and turn away. Surely, we are not like him! Yet I have to admit that too many times his face eerily resembles mine.

People outside God's family by choice should see themselves in the older brother. If we are standing outside the joyous celebration that is salvation and life with God, we do so because we are self-excluded. He wants everyone to join the party; His invitation is universal. All through the Scriptures, God's invitation is extended. "I have set before your life and death, blessings and curses. Now choose life, so that you and your children may live" (Deut. 30:19). "Come, all you who are thirsty, come to the waters; and you who have no money, come, buy and eat! Come, buy wine and milk without money and without cost" (Isa. 55:1). "I take no pleasure in the death of anyone, declares the Sovereign Lord. Repent and live!" (Ezek. 18:32). Jesus said, "Come to me, all you who are weary and burdened, and I will give you rest. Take my yoke upon you and learn from me, for I am gentle and humble in heart, and you will find rest for your souls. For my yoke is easy and my burden is light" (Matt. 11:28-30). John wrote, "The Spirit and the bride say, 'Come!' And let him who hears say, 'Come!' Whoever is thirsty, let him come; and whoever wishes, let him take the free gift of the water of life" (Rev. 22:17). God invites us to come to Him; we choose to accept or reject His invitation to join Him in celebration.

In Jesus' final scene is the vivid truth that sin is a barrier to relationship with God. He removes the barrier when we confess our sins, repent of them, and place our faith in Christ. No less a barrier is self-generated goodness—self-righteousness based on good works that causes us to feel we deserve right standing with God. We reach a dangerous point when we feel God owes us something because of our good works. Such perceived goodness also creates a barrier that separates self-styled "good" people from others viewed as sinful or inferior. Thus, goodness seen as earned can separate us from God and others.

As was the older brother, we can be judgmental of people who do not live by our standards. I have to confess that too often I am swift to claim grace for myself while wanting others to receive justice as I perceive it. I have been helped to see that merely because others do not live by my standards is no grounds for rejecting them.

I find the older brother's sarcastic, biting accusation that his younger brother had consumed his father's livelihood with prostitutes to be instructive and indicting. I am among those who believe the older brother assumed the prodigal engaged in immoral activity. If so, he assumed the worst about his brother. This is one attitude we can take toward others we do not like or who are not like us. We can make negative assumptions that make us look good by comparison and/or make us feel better about ourselves.

An advancement on the attitude of assuming the worst is to give others the benefit of the doubt. We can reserve judgment until we have more information and assume people are "innocent until they are proved guilty."

A third attitude we can take toward others is the one Jesus modeled. He looked for the best in people and sought to bring it to the forefront. If a spark of good existed in a person, though it may have been covered with layers of trash and debris, He found it and sought to fan it into flame.

By assuming the worst, the self-righteous older brother missed a chance to help in his brother's recovery. Before I can judge him and feel better about myself, I must ask myself: *How do I approach people around me and individuals I meet daily? What is my dominant attitude in relating to others?* Too often, I am not comfortable with the answers.

In the father's response to the older brother is a truth previously noted. As God's children by faith, we have access to His gracious and generous provisions. We live in His lavish grace and love. We can be assured of His faithful care in all life's experiences. We have the gift of His presence and the assurance of uninterrupted life with Him. We can celebrate our relationship with Him and the relationship others have with Him.

Jesus' vivid word picture in the mural's fifth scene teaches that we must have a healthy understanding of what being God's children means and must value that relationship. A great danger God's children face is taking that status for granted. We must guard against losing a deep sense of awe and wonder that God would want us as His children, make a way for us into His family, and receive us when we approach Him. Indeed, we are children of the King, the Creator of the universe whose essence is love. We can be grateful that He does not give up on us easily but continues His merciful, gracious overtures. Neither son in Jesus' story had a firm grasp on the meaning of sonship. Perhaps the returning prodigal had come to understand something of the meaning and significance of his relationship with his father. Evidently the older brother failed to see clearly what being his father's son meant.

The two sons' relationship with their father poses a crucial question for us: What does being God's sons—God's children—mean? First and foremost, it means He is our Father in the absolute best sense of that word. He is delighted to have us as His children. That God would want us in His family and would spare no effort or expense to Himself to include us is an amazing truth beyond my comprehension. His doing so remains a mystery to me. Why would He want us when nothing in us merits His love and grace? Yet His deep longing is to have all people join His family. Paul used the analogy of adoption to stress the incredible truth that God takes the initiative to bring us into His family. (See Rom. 8:15 ["sonship" literally is "adoption"]; Rom. 8:23; Gal. 4:4-5 ["full rights of sons" literally is "the adoption"]; and Eph. 1:5.)

As noted earlier, the writer of 1 John captured the almost unbelievable excitement generated by the realization that people who have placed their faith in Christ are God's children: "How great is the love the Father has lavished on us, that we should be called children of God! And that is what we are!" (1 John 3:1).

Second, being God's children means we can trust ourselves to His care in the assurance that He loves us. He wants the best for us and constantly works toward that end. He gently but firmly guides us toward spiritual maturity. He is faithful and generous in His provision for us. Out of His grace, He gives us what we need to meet the challenges and demands of our living. I am convinced He does not give us all we want; He gives us all we need to enable us to grow into His likeness and to serve Him effectively.

Third, as God's children we can be confident His compassion for us never wanes. More deeply that our feeble words can express, He feels with us in our pain. Whether we suffer because of our sins, others' sins, or factors and circumstances over which we have no control, He suffers with us and works for our good. No matter how abandoned we may feel in times of great difficulty, we are never alone. Nothing can separate us from God's love for us (see Rom. 8:35-39).

From our standpoint, being God's children involves certain responses to Him. The first of these is to love Him. When Jesus was asked which command is the greatest, He said, "Love the Lord your God with all your heart and with all your soul and with all your mind" (Matt. 22:37). He declared that closely tied to the command to love God totally is the command to "love your neighbor as yourself" (Matt. 22:39). First, we are to love God with our whole selves—with the same kind of love He has for us, and we are to love His other children.

Second, we are to obey the Father. We are to keep His commands as revealed in the Scriptures. John wrote: "This is love for God: to obey his commands. And his commands are not burdensome" (1 John 5:3). Children who truly love their Heavenly Father want to do what He has said and what He continues to express through His presence in our lives. We obey, not out of fear or to court His favor in pursuit of selfish desires, but because we love Him supremely.

Third, we who are God's children want to please Him. We want to experience His smile of approval. The natural tendency is to please ourselves or to please others so we can win their approval or gain favors from them. In our relationship with our Father, we seek His approval, for His opinion is the only one that ultimately counts with us.

In Jesus' beatitudes in Matthew 5:3-12, He contrasted the world's view of certain characteristics with God's view of those qualities. The Greek word commonly translated "blessed" *(makarios)* does not mean "happy"; it has the sense of "to be congratulated." Jesus said that in God's evaluation of people, the disciple who is poor in spirit, who mourns, who is meek, who hungers and thirsts for righteousness, who is merciful, who is pure in heart, who is a peacemaker, and who is persecuted because of righteousness receives God's congratulations, for that person is on the right track in life. God's evaluation ultimately is the only assessment that matters.

In Colossians 1:10-12, Paul gave his readers ways to "please [the Lord] in every way" (v. 10). They were to bear the fruit of good works, to grow "in the knowledge of God," to be strengthened by God's power so they could endure and have patience, and to give thanks to the Father with joy (vv. 10-12).

The writer of Hebrews admonished Christians to "continually offer to God a sacrifice of praise—the fruit of lips that confess his name. And do not forget to do good and to share with others, for with such sacrifices God is pleased."

Of course, neither list is exhaustive. For example, we please God when we love and serve one another, build strong family bonds, and help strengthen fellowship in the community of faith.

Fourth, out of our love for our Father, we are to seek to honor Him. We do so by lifestyles that reflect His character. In Jesus' parable, the younger son dishonored his father by the son's impetuous request, by turning his back on his father, by squandering the father's money, and by sinking to the depths of a pig pen. The elder son dishonored his father by his attitude toward the father's graciousness, his harsh words and stinging accusations directed against the father, and his refusal to go in to the banquet and greet his brother. God's children dishonor Him when their words and actions arise out of self-centeredness, self-trust, and self-will rather than out of faithfulness to His lordship. We honor Him by resembling Him in character.

To be God's children is a great gift of sheer love. With the gift comes the demand to love, obey, please, honor, and serve Him. Helmut Thielicke wrote: "It can be the death of our faith if we forget that it is literally a miracle, a gift, an absolutely-not-to-be-taken-for-granted fact that we are able to say, 'Abba, Father,' and 'My Lord and my God.' "[20] We must not allow our status as God's children to become a point of pride. The realization that God claims us as His children is humbling and challenging, and it should be a focus of continuing gratitude.

---

[20] Thielicke, 34.

In the exchange between the father and his older son, Jesus clearly taught that we cannot be related to God properly if we are not related rightly to others. Even if others reject us and our expressions of good will, we are to remain open and caring. As believers, relationship with others is not a minor part of our living, and it is not an option. We all are God's creatures and bear His image; because He values every person, so must we. That means we must be willing to invest in others' lives. Every time a person separated from God turns to Him and home, we must receive the individual with open arms and hearts. We must join in celebrating God's great love and grace that receives sinners. We must celebrate His amazingly deep compassion that reaches out to include everyone. Celebration is the only right response.

Leaving the story of the compassionate father open-ended, Jesus turned to His disciples and told them a story about a dishonest manager. His point to His followers was that they were to be as shrewd, innovative, and enterprising in ministry for Him as the dishonest manager was in providing for his future. The Pharisees, who were still present, heard the story and Jesus' teachings about money that followed. Jesus said emphatically, "You cannot serve God and money" (16:13). "The Pharisees, who loved money, heard all this and were sneering at Jesus" (v. 14). In 16:15-31, Jesus continued His attempts to penetrate the Pharisees' religious armor. He did not give up easily on these self-righteous people who needed God's grace as much as the tax collectors and sinners did.

Scene 6: _____

The Compassionate Father

In the fifth scene of Jesus' mural of the compassionate father and his two sons, the father stands outside the house. Inside, a party is in full swing. Tenderly and lovingly, the father entreats his older son to go inside and join the celebration of his younger brother's return. The father wants the incensed elder brother to be a true son and compassionate brother. In a real sense, the father seeks to reclaim his other lost son.

We move to face the last scene of Jesus mural and view a blank space prepared for work. By design, Jesus' story of the father with two sons leaves us hanging; it is incomplete. The Lord deliberately left it open-ended. We are left to consider how the verbal mural might be completed. Spread before the sixth scene is an array of brushes. Palates are laden with paints in a wide variety of colors. The last scene remains to be painted. For a moment, we stare in surprise, perplexed by the unfinished work.

Jesus invites—even demands—that we paint the last scene in His mural. Now, my artistic ability is limited to stick figures, at best awkwardly drawn. I smile when I see the TV commercial that has been running for years in which a spokesman for an art school invites viewers to send for a simple art test that may demonstrate latent talent for painting. Doubtless my sample drawing would elicit a "you've-got-to-be-kidding" reply and would be posted in a conspicuous place as a running art joke. Yet however we complete Jesus' mural, our work in doing so is crucial.

Jesus' story forever answers any question people may have about what God is like and how He approaches us. The earthly father's inclusive compassion for both his sons and his dealings with them mirror God's unfathomable love for every person. He works untiringly for our good. We can count on His compassion.

Jesus' story, however, leaves unanswered questions. Our questions concern the two sons. Before we jump to consider definitive questions about the older brother's response, we need to focus on the restored younger son. What had he learned from his painful experience in the far country? Did he acquire and maintain a healthy understanding of his father? With what attitude did he approach his relationship with his father in the days after his return? How did his father's reception affect him? Did he approach his work alongside his father with a new, fresh enthusiasm? Did gratitude fuel his determination to please his father? How had his understanding of sonship changed? How did he relate to his older brother? These and other questions arise out of the younger son's experiences.

For the sinners and tax collectors who had responded positively to God's love and grace that Jesus offered them, the question would concern their manner of life as God's children. In sharp contrast to their former lifestyles, they now were called to live in godly morality and ethical behavior. They were to live by the standards of God's kingdom and were to reflect their Heavenly Father's character. Their lives were to be marked by gratitude, obedience, and spiritual growth.

Although we do not have answers to the questions about the younger son, the questions hang in the air as we contemplate the mural's final, blank space; and they force us to ask them of ourselves. What have we learned about sin and self-will from once being separated from God? Have we acquired and maintained a healthy understanding of our Heavenly Father? With what attitude do we approach our relationship with Him since we have experienced His love and grace? How has God's receiving us warmly and openly in life-changing forgiveness affected us? Do we approach our work for and with our Father with renewed enthusiasm and vigor? Does gratitude fuel our determination to please the Father? How has our understanding of being God's children changed and grown? How are we relating to our brothers and sisters in God's family?

Questions remain concerning the older son in Jesus' story. Did the Pharisees and scribes see themselves in the figure of the older brother in Jesus' mural? If so, how did they react? Did the older brother relent and join the celebration? Did the religious leaders change their attitudes and accept sinners and tax collectors as brothers? Even more importantly, did the religious leaders' attitude toward Jesus and His representation of God change?

Again, we do not have answers to questions concerning the older son and the religious leaders he represented. Yet questions about him and them become questions about us. Do we see something of ourselves in the older brother—something of his self-justification, lack of love and forgiveness, self-righteousness, and smug superiority? If so, what are we doing to remove the similarities? Do we share God's great joy at people's coming home to Him? Do we extend open acceptance to all other Christians?

Some interpreters have written that the older brother remained outside through stubborn choice. They maintain that as a whole, the Jews' religious leaders opted not to join God's celebration of sinners coming to Him through faith in Christ. Some religious leaders did accept Jesus, but the vast majority clung to Judaism and works of the law. In the course of time, a split occurred between the church and the synagogue. Some Jews who became Christians asserted that believing Gentiles had to become Jewish proselytes in addition to placing faith in Christ. This resulted in the Jerusalem Conference (Acts 15), which decreed that Gentiles became Christians through faith in Christ alone. Still, Paul had to go on defending the good news of salvation by grace through faith in Christ because Jewish Christians continued to demand that male Gentile converts be circumcised and that all converts keep Jewish regulations.

My guess is that the majority of people who read and hear Jesus' parable identify most readily with the prodigal. They willingly admit that they once were sinners separated from God by choice. Then they came to themselves, repented, and experienced God's glad welcome. They are still sinners, but in fellowship with God they grow toward spiritual maturity.

Most of us are extremely reluctant to identify with the older brother. Surely we are not that legalistic, unforgiving, self-righteous, and joyless! Yet in any number of ways, we can view ourselves as superior to others; deep down, we can feel we are more deserving of God's love than others whom we consider to be not as good as we are. We can revel in grace and yet can be graceless. Emil Brunner wrote: "The parable mentions two different people, the younger brother who went away and the elder one who stayed home. But as we meditate on this parable, we are both; now we resemble more the one son, now more the other."[1]

If you were the younger brother in Jesus' story, what would you paint as the sixth scene in the mural as an ending to the story? If you were the older brother—outside on the porch while a party your Father has invited you to attend is in progress inside—what final scene of the mural would you be able to paint? J. Stanley Glen issued a chilling warning to religious people prone to self-congratulations: "Since . . . there is no hint of the elder brother's

---

[1] Brunner, 35.

ever being reconciled to the father and to the prodigal, the suggestion will remain that such failure as a form of opposition to the graciousness of God within religion is more dangerous than the escape from God into irreligion."[2]

In answering His critics by telling the parable of the loving father, Jesus clearly and simply portrayed God's great love, mercy, grace, and forgiveness. No frowning Deity, God is the Father of deep compassion, hugs, kisses, lavish kindness, and tender entreaty. The people of Jesus' day needed this revelation of God given in Jesus' acceptance of all people. They needed the assurance that God is not a scowling, capricious Deity bent on punishment. To be sure, people's rejection of the Father's love issues in self-judgment, self-indictment. God's intention, however, is that every person turn to Him, to home. Jesus' story of the loving Father calls for all people truly to be at home in His Father's house.

Jesus' story is an invitation and a warning. It invites all people to realize God loves them and wants them to be members of His family. Though our sins have rendered us unacceptable, God in His grace accepts us. Leon Morris wrote, "That Jesus leaves the elder brother's reaction open is encouraging. We can still do the right thing. God's love is a continuing challenge to all our self-seeking."[3]

The story conveys a somber warning: Relationship with the Father demands relationship with others—an openness to accept and love others no matter how unlovely they may seem to be. We cannot claim His grace and refuse to extend it to others. We cannot luxuriate in His love and be loveless in dealing with others. We cannot receive His compassion and fail to be compassionate.

Jesus told a beautiful story unmatched in the long history of storytelling. Actually, we must use the present tense rather than the past tense. The resurrected Jesus tells the story now, here, for our response. John Claypool expressed this truth in the title of his book on some of Jesus' parables: *Stories Jesus Still Tells*. Gunter Bornkamm insightfully pointed out that the early Christians did not view Jesus' words as teachings in the past but as present pronouncements. Bornkamm wrote: "To the original Christian tradition, Jesus is not in the first instance a figure of the past, but rather the risen Lord, present with his will, his power, his word. . . .

---

[2] Glen, 39.
[3] Morris, 245.

Because the earthly Jesus is for the church at the same time the Risen Lord, his word takes on, in the tradition, the features of the present. . . . The tradition is not really the repetition and transmission of the word he spoke once upon a time but rather *is* his word today."[4]

So, the Parable of the Compassionate Father is more than an attractive, compelling story out of the past but is the resurrected Christ's word for today. Every time we read it or hear it, it calls for us to make decisions. It forces us to ask ourselves, *Have I sought and received the Father's forgiving grace? If so, what kind of child am I? Have I tried to separate my relationship with God from my relationships with others? Has my smug trust in my own goodness caused me to be judgmental of others, holding them at arms' length?* The answers to such questions are crucial. They are life-determining. Each time we read or hear the world's greatest unfinished short story, the risen, living Storyteller compels us to answer penetrating questions: What ending are we writing to His haunting story? What final scene in His matchless mural are we painting?

---

[4] Gunter Bornkamm, *Jesus of Nazareth* (New York: Harper & Row, 1960), 16-17.

Selected Bibliography

Barclay, William, *And Jesus Said* (Edinburgh: The Church of Scotland Youth Committee, 1966)

_____*More New Testament Words* (New York: Harper & Row, Publishers, 1960)

Bornkamm, Gunter, *Jesus of Nazareth* (New York: Harper & Rowe, Publishers, 1960)

Brooks, James A., "Mark," in *The New American Commentary*, vol. 23 (Nashville: Broadman Press, 1991)

Brunner, Emil, *Sowing and Reaping: The Parables of Jesus* (Richmond: John Knox Press, 1965)

Buttrick, George A., *The Parables of Jesus* (New Your: Harper & Row, Publishers, 1928)

_____, "The Gospel According to St. Luke" in *The Interpreter's Bible*, vol. 8 (Nashville: Broadman Press, 1952)

Cargill, Robert L., *All the Parables of Jesus* (Nashville: Broadman Press, 1970)

Claypool, John, *Stories Jesus Still Tells: The Parables* (Cambridge: Cowley Publications, 2000)

_____, *The Saga of Life: Living Gracefully Through all of the Stages* (New Orleans: Insight Press, 2003)

Dean, Robert J., "Luke" in *Layman's Bible Book Commentary*, vol. 17 (Nashville: Broadman Press, 1983)

Faber, Frederick W., "There's a Wideness in God's Mercy" in *The Baptist Hymnal* (Nashville: Convention Press, 1991)

Fitzmyer, Joseph A., "The Gospel According to Luke X-XXV" in *The Anchor Bible*, vol. 28a (Garden City, New York: Doubleday & Company, Inc., 1985)

Geldenhuys, Norval, "Commentary on the Gospel of Luke" in *The New International Commentary on the New Testament* (Grand Rapids, Michigan: Wm. B. Eerdmans Publishing Company, 1960)

Glen, J. Stanley, *The Parables of Conflict in Luke* (Philadelphia: The Westminster Press, 1962

Green, Joel B., "The Gospel of Luke" in *The New International Commentary on the New Testament* (Grand Rapids, Michigan: Wm. B. Eerdmans Publishing Company, 1997)
Holman Christian Standard Bible (Nashville: Holman Bible Publishers, 2004)

Hunter, Archibald M., *Interpreting the Parables* (Philadelphia: The Westminster Press, 1960)

_____, *The Parables Then and Now* (Philadelphia: The Westminster Press, 1971)

Jeremias, Joachim, *The Parables of Jesus* (London: SCM Press LTD, 1963)

_____, *Rediscovering the Parables* (London: SCM Press LTD, 1966)

Jordan, Clarence, *The Cotton Patch Version of Luke and Acts* (New York: Association Press, 1969

L" Amour, Louis, *Riding for the Brand* (New York: Bantam Books, 1986)

Lenski, R. C. H., *The Interpretation of St. Luke's Gospel* (Columbus, Ohio: The Wartburg Press, 1946)

Marshall, I. Howard, "The Gospel of Luke: A Commentary on the Greek Text" in The

New International Greek Testament Commentary (Grand Rapids, Michigan: William B. Eerdmans Publishing Company, 1978)

Morris, Leon, "The Gospel According to St. Luke" in *Tyndale Bible Commentaries* (Grand Rapids, Michigan: William B. Eerdmans Publishing Company, 1974)

Nolland, John, "Luke 9:21—18:34" in *Word Biblical Commentary*, vol. 35b (Dallas, Texas: Word Books, Publisher, 1993)

Owens, J. Garfield, *All God's Chillun: Meditations on Negro Spirituals* (Nashville: Abingdon Press, 1971)

Phillips, J. B., *The Gospels in Modern English* (New York: The McMillan Company, 1954)

Plummer, Alfred, "A Critical and Exegetical Commentary on the Gospel According to S. Luke" in *The International Critical Commentary* (Edinburgh: T. & T. Clark, 1964)

Robertson, Archibald Thomas, "The Gospel According to Luke" in *Word Pictures in the New Testament,* vol. II (Nashville: Broadman Press, 1930)

Stagg, Frank, *Studies in Luke's Gospel* (Nashville: Convention Press, 1967)

Stein, Robert H., "Luke" in *The New American Commentary,* vol. 24 (Nashville: Broadman Press, 1992)

The Amplified New Testament (Grand Rapids: Zondervan Publishing House, 1958)

The Analytical Greek Lexicon (New York: Harper & Row, Publishers, nd)

Thielicke, Helmut, The Waiting Father (New York: Harper & Row, Publishers, 1959)

Thompson, Will I., "Softly and Tenderly" in *The Baptist Hymnal* (Nashville: Convention Press, 1991)

Tolbert, Malcolm O., "Luke" in *The Broadman Bible Commentary*, vol. 9 (Nashville: Broadman Press, 1970)

Trench, R. C., *Notes on the Parables of our Lord* (Grand Rapids, Michigan: Baker Book House, 1948)

Vincent, Marvin R., "The Gospel According to Luke" in *Word Studies in the New Testament*, vol. 1 (Grand Rapids, Michigan: Wm B. Eerdmans Publishing Company, 1965)

Weatherhead, Leslie D., *Over His Own Signature* (London: Epworth Press, 1960)

_____, *In Quest of a Kingdom* (Nashville: Abingdon Press, 1944)

Webster's New World Dictionary of the American Language: College Edition (Cleveland: The World Publishing Company, 1964)

Williams, Charles B., *The New Testament in the Language of the People* (Nashville: Holman Bible Publishers, 1986)

www.ingramcontent.com/pod-product-compliance
Lightning Source LLC
Chambersburg PA
CBHW071521080526
44588CB00011B/1516